Murder at the Met

Murder at the Met

EDWARD GRAY

iUniverse

MURDER AT THE MET

Copyright © 2017 Edward Gray.

All rights reserved. No part of this book may be used or reproduced by any means, graphic, electronic, or mechanical, including photocopying, recording, taping or by any information storage retrieval system without the written permission of the author except in the case of brief quotations embodied in critical articles and reviews.

This is a work of fiction. All of the characters, names, incidents, organizations, and dialogue in this novel are either the products of the author's imagination or are used fictitiously.

iUniverse books may be ordered through booksellers or by contacting:

iUniverse
1663 Liberty Drive
Bloomington, IN 47403
www.iuniverse.com
1-800-Authors (1-800-288-4677)

Because of the dynamic nature of the Internet, any web addresses or links contained in this book may have changed since publication and may no longer be valid. The views expressed in this work are solely those of the author and do not necessarily reflect the views of the publisher, and the publisher hereby disclaims any responsibility for them.

Any people depicted in stock imagery provided by Thinkstock are models, and such images are being used for illustrative purposes only. Certain stock imagery © Thinkstock.

ISBN: 978-1-5320-1840-4 (sc)
ISBN: 978-1-5320-1841-1 (e)

Library of Congress Control Number: 2017903468

Print information available on the last page.

iUniverse rev. date: 04/19/2017

CHAPTER 1

So damned inconsiderate! Head slumped on his chest and sound asleep before the first aria.

The orchestra almost fully seated. Soon it would be time for his grand entrance: the Conductor making his way through the orchestra pit from stage right. He who is absolutely adored for his handsome countenance as enhanced by a well-groomed, long white mane and matching Van Dyke beard. An image complemented by his usual long string tie. I am told that it is even worn when he is in bed.

That total picture always produces a very audible female-voice register chorus of Oohs and Aahs.

Man, that distinguished baton-wielding dude we all know from fan magazines sure looked the part!

Probably just a pretty boy they found in central casting. I hope he at least remembered to bring his notes.

All of this happened in the final few seconds as the remaining stragglers found their seats.

That snoozing slob in the next seat did not even acknowledge my presence and was still slumped in his seat. Not even appropriately dressed for THE Opera (read, THE METROPOLITAN Opera). Chinos and a striped sports polo shirt. Probably a three-dollar knock-off from some Bangkok strip mall. What's this? Is it a marinara stain on the front of his shirt? Marinara? Isn't that some kind of foreign sauce-y thing? It sounds kind of "Eye-talian."

Don't those people know anything about or even begin to appreciate how important THE opera is?

More importantly, are they even aware that proper dress is absolutely mandated? I'm sure that it is in the by-laws for these seats. Hmm, must have Maurice check that out! Especially when it is this Verdi guy, the one who wrote the "Thingy" tonight. His name even sounds "Eye-talian."

What's gives with this guy next to me? A total loser. At least he's not snoring, coughing or farting.

Her bleached beehive of towering, sort-of blondish straw hair teetered like an incoming tsunami as she sneeringly said, "EXCUSE ME," at least three times, before resorting to squeeeezing the obviously expensive green and yellow massive silk tent that covered her ever so abundant rump, around his partially slumped form.

The inconsiderate slob is obviously under the influence of a lot too many or it could even be, just possibly, the result of a really hard day at the office. Neither excuse even remotely acceptable at THE Opera, especially among the $500+ extracted by management for each of these premium seats. $500, even though I am a major donor," she thought. *"The nerve. I must get Maurice to check into that as well."*

The audience of 3,800, plus 195 standees, an absolutely full house expected tonight, continued to trickle in at an ever-increasing pace. At two minutes to eight, as is the eagerly anticipated custom, the house lights gradually dimmed and that always-exciting Metropolitan Opera House pre-performance extravaganza was about to begin.

Those magnificent crystal chandeliers, the centerpieces of the hall, would be raised to the ceiling. Ornate chandeliers have been the centerpiece of major opera houses around the world since the era of candlelight. These particular majestic centerpieces had been created by the esteemed J & L Lobmeyr House of Vienna and donated to The Met in 1966 by the Austrian Government in gratitude for the US Marshall Plan funding of the restoration of the Vienna State Opera House after its destruction in WWII. What a wonderful gift, enjoyed and appreciated almost every night of the past 50 years of the Met Opera (and Ballet) Seasons in their then new home at the Lincoln Center complex.

The central 1 1/2-ton chandelier some 18 feet wide, with its 260 brilliant bulbs arranged in a starburst pattern (nicknamed "Sputnik"), surrounded by 20 smaller satellite companions, were all about to be raised some sixty-five feet to the ceiling. The white lights, in concert (how appropriate a term in this hall) with some 300 wall sconces lighting the auditorium, simultaneously and gradually dimmed during their ascent.

Arthur Millstein had just pushed the appropriate buttons on his backstage, stage left, control panel for the 2,674[th] time in his 17 years as the chief Met electrician. There were no particular reasons to expect any problems this evening, especially on the night his favorite opera was about to begin.

Rigoletto was as good as it gets, certainly the best of Giuseppe Verdi's 27 operas. It not only got Art's attention, but resonated to his very core. His heartbeat echoed the opening chords.

Throughout each performance, his inner being was transformed into the Duke of Mantua seeking, but never quite reaching, his Gilda. Art imitated Art which imitated life, or was it life imitating art? Art (the real one), an eternal bachelor of some 49 years, was still seeking his real-life mate.

Unfortunately, the only women he had met to date never looked like his idealized Gilda. Come to think of it, the introverted skinny and bald Art never looked quite like the heroic Duke.

Enough ruminating. Back to the buttons.

High above the auditorium's gilt ceiling, twenty-one synchronized motors responded to his fingertip commands, powering the winches that seemed to float the Prima Ballerina and her Corps de Ballet on their journey. The twenty small satellite chandeliers, along with the grand central star of this show within a show, began their one-minute trip towards the heavens of this magnificent hall.

Forty-nine thousand Venetian leaded-crystal pendants showered the hall with faint rainbow arcs, as smiling heads tilted up to follow this almost holy ascent of ROYGBIV (come on, you must remember your high school physics lessons on the color composition of light) dancing across the curtain.

Art, respecting his years of diligence and technical training, carefully watched the individual ammeters to monitor the motor's electrical loads. With hundreds of people directly beneath each chandelier, this responsibility was always taken very seriously. There was no way that

Art could allow any malfunction of these heavy potential bombs to go unaddressed.

In 17 years, he had never missed a performance. The only major problem he had ever had to deal with was that one night in 1992 when there was the citywide power failure two hours before the opening curtain. You may remember that evening. The subways came to a screeching halt with only the eerie yellowish emergency lights casting frightening shadows. Traffic came to a dead stop as all of the street lighting and traffic lights failed. Elevators in tall buildings trapped their passengers for many, many hours, resulting in a record birth rate in New York City some nine months later.

The position of Art's chandeliers at that time was almost a non-issue as compared to the citywide problems. However, the phasing in of his emergency generators to allow the performance to go on that night was paramount to him.

I am quite sure it was *The Barber of Seville* that night.

I remember that was the night when the poor barber of Seville shaved his customer while resorting to his bifocals, and a flashlight to illuminate the wary Don's face. I believe it was as a result of that performance that the great tenor, Nicholas Politus, earned the sobriquet "Nick the Greek."

Art's eyes widened, as he was unexpectedly jerked back to the present moment. The hallowed hall on the other side of the curtain echoed with a terrified, very non-operatic scream. It was a pure John Cage note, high L, I think. At least it sounded like L! The magnificent acoustics of the hall further amplified this horrible sound as it rebounded throughout the entire building. Within milliseconds it was followed by the high-pitched screeches of an equal cacophony-of-sounds chorus, all emanating from somewhere in the center of the auditorium.

Art's eyes further widened and his lower lip dropped as he watched the central chandelier ammeter jump from its normal 360 amps into the broad, bright-red upper limit line to 420 amps, clearly indicating some sort of major problem.

This had never happened before.

Art responded instinctively and immediately turned off the power to all of the motors until he could analyze and then rectify the situation.

The screaming intensified.

He peered out from behind the curtain and saw people in the hall's center seats clearly in a panic, yelling and running toward the aisles. There was no "Excuse me," "Pardon me," or any such nicety. Just "Get the hell out of my way." It was not quite mayhem. Although people obviously wanted out, they were still slowed down by the ones in front of them.

Figures clutching fur coats and large purses flew away from what appeared at first glance to be a human form, dangling by its neck, some 10-12 feet above the seats.

A second glance did not change that perception.

There was no question but that there was a body hanging directly under the central chandelier.

Art's reaction was instantaneous. He reversed the motors to once again lower all of them.

The fire, police, medical and security people that NY State requires to be in attendance at every major public gathering, raced toward the cause of the frenzy. They were running countercurrent to the flow of the crowded aisles, but still managed to get there within one minute of the first scream.

Officer Oswald Franklin arrived at just about the same time as Dr. William Pearl. They watched in horror as the descending chandelier lowered the body once again, slumping it back into its seat, K-126.

He still was not snoring, coughing or farting.

Dr. Pearl immediately reached for the victim's neck to check for a pulse.

No pulse.

No heartbeat.

No respiration.

No more.

During the course of his initial touch to the victim's neck, Dr. Pearl noticed the almost totally invisible nylon cord wrapped around the neck leading up to the chandelier. Using Officer Franklin's pocketknife to sever it, he once again checked for vital signs before pronouncing him.

Yes, it was a he.

And he was dead.

Dr. Pearl, who some eight years earlier had completed his residency in internal medicine at Beth Israel Hospital and had then worked in the New York City Medical Examiner's Office for four years, was experienced enough to know that this poor guy was beyond help. Dr. Pearl's part-time pro-bono work at the Met was a way for him to indulge his great passion for the opera, gratis. It was usually an uninterrupted paradise for him.

Tonight was going to be different, very different.

He was more than earning his non-salary.

Dr. Pearl made an educated guess as to the time of death, based on the usual preliminary parameters: rigor mortis, color, body temperature, odor, skin tone, etc. Rigidity and skin color indicated that the John Doe had been dead for at least five hours, well before being "hanged" by the chandelier. The stain on his shirt was certainly not blood, but probably some sort of food dripping, possibly marinara sauce. There obviously had to be another cause of death, which would only be revealed by a post mortem.

Without missing a beat, Officer Franklin automatically went into his well-trained professional overdrive. He called for a PA announcement to be made ordering the evacuation of the area, indeed, the entire hall. All attendees were also required to remain in the lobby until questioned and released by the Police Department. He then stationed all of the extra emergency people and Met personnel to cover each exit to ensure that no one left the building before reinforcements arrived.

Three months later, Officer Franklin was awarded a Departmental Commendation recognizing his cool-headed and professional response.

911 recorded 162 calls, all but two from cell phones, within three minutes of the first scream. The General Manager's Office had also immediately called the police and EMS, as had the other individual officers on duty at the scene.

All of the above took about seven minutes.

CHAPTER 2

He routed the incoming call to the squawk box so that he could write while listening.

"Yes Lieutenant, I was at the rear of the auditorium checking the incoming faces, dress and possessions, looking for the out-of-place, the nervous glances and the other tell-tales we've been trained to look for. No luggage, large parcels or bags were allowed in. Nothing special caught my attention."

"Go on."

Referring to his notes, Franklin continued, "At 7:58, a woman screamed, followed by full-scale panic. People rushed away from the center of the hall. I ran down the right aisle to row K and saw the John Doe about 12 seats in and dangling some 10 feet high. In accordance with our emergency protocol, I ordered all building exits sealed. The house physician, a Dr. William Pearl, was right behind me. After the chandelier was lowered, we cut off the plastic noose and Dr. Pearl, the duty MD, examined and pronounced."

"Thanks, Franklin. Report to Sgt. Bailey in the lobby and stay available."

Lt. Cornelius Collins, 39 years old, a Grade-1 Detective, NYPD Homicide Division, was at his 7th Precinct duty desk when the calls started coming in. His angular face had lines etched into it that seemed to represent every corpse seen in his 17 years on the force, the last 11 of which were worked in homicide. He didn't need his Walgreen's 125+ reading glasses to recite *The Department Response Book*. After all those years he knew them by heart, and didn't waste a second. The phone never returned to its base as Connie called for:

uniformed backup
taping off of the entire Met plaza
sealing all entrances to the opera house, with all attendees and personnel inside
homicide and forensic specialists
Medical Examiner.

"Lebowitz, find Stone and Watkins and get there yesterday. Lisa, call the garage and tell them I need my car, then the Mayor's office and tell them we have a code 16 at The Met. Next, find the Captain and tell him I'm on my way to the opera. No time to change into my tux."

The four flights of stairs leading to the station's underground garage were negotiated two steps at a time, not quite meeting his personal best record of 48 seconds. His dark blue 2015 Ford Fairlane sedan was already at the base of the stairwell with Billings behind the wheel.

Connie jumped into the passenger seat yelling, "Why aren't we there yet?"

Midtown traffic was, as usual this time of evening, miserable, however their siren and red/blue lights managed to clear a path. Six minutes later the car screeched to a stop and Connie bounded up both of the two steps leading to the Lincoln Center Plaza in front of The Met.

Two nights a week spent at the department gym paid off like a slot machine.

A uniform just outside the main entrance yelled, "Lieutenant, over here."

After Franklin's more detailed briefing brought him up to speed, Connie barked orders to the assembled uniformed sergeants and detectives.

The uniforms were to organize crowd control and take all names and addresses, and check picture ID's. The detectives were to question those closest to the chandelier first and get to the others later.

Satisfied that the lobby was secure, Connie followed Franklin into the auditorium, down the center right aisle, to Row K.

There must have been ten or twelve officials and uniforms at the scene.

"All right now. Can you all stop what you are doing for a few minutes and move out of the way so that I can have a clear view of the scene? C'mon now, that includes you with the tape.

Officer is that your bag or was it found here?"

"Sorry sir, that's my forensics kit. I'll get it out of the way."

There were no obvious wounds nor were there bloodstains or other bodily fluids on the deceased, the seat, or carpet beneath. He had obviously been a goner long before being deposited in K 126.

After a few minutes, the forensics team was given the go-ahead by Connie and continued to dust for fingerprints and carried out a minute examination of the surrounding area.

Once the techies completed their inspection and sampling, Connie reached into the victim's pants pocket to look for identification. He always checked the right side-pocket first.

It used to be the rear right pocket first, because that was where most men kept their wallets. Some twenty years ago men began to realize that every time they sat down, their super thick wallets were throwing their hips out of alignment. Chiropractors are expensive. Experience through the years taught Connie that that's when the wallets moved to the side.

"Bingo, got it.

Maleski, I count $842. Please confirm, bag it and so note. Also note John Doe's info on his driver's license.

It's his. The license photo is a dead match. Sorry about that, it just came out that way.

His name was Enrico Calzoni, 422 Central Park West, Apt. 28H, New York, NY 10010.

Bailey, why aren't you at his residence yet? See if there is a next-of-kin to inform and confirm the ID. If no answer, make sure you have a warrant to enter, check and seal.

What are you waiting for? Go.

Watkins."

"Over here sir."

"Call the station. Get anything they can dig up on Enrico Calzoni. Also, get them to issue a warrant to enter the deceased's property, and get it to Bailey."

Connie mused that it would clarify things if Mr. Calzoni was an opera singer, a Mafia soldier or both. How about a Mafia singer? That <u>would</u> be a clear motive!

Even more sinister, he may have been a lawyer.

Connie spoke to Dr. Pearl, "OK, Doc. Fill me in."

Pearl looked at his notes and said, "It appears that he has been dead for at least five hours, however the timing will be confirmed after the Medical Examiner has had an opportunity to examine the body. I feel relatively safe in saying that it was not caused by strangulation. There are no visible reddened neck bruises and the larynx seems to be intact. An immediate anomaly is that his coloration is not pallid, but is the blue usually associated with asphyxiation.

I would bet two box seats that the hanging did not contribute to his demise and was probably only for the dramatic impact. After all, we are at the opera. No question about it, this is absolutely a dramatic setup to make some sort of statement!

Beyond an obvious murder, what is he trying to tell us?"

CHAPTER 3

"No, no, no, Elaine! Your *veebrato* must come from deep *weethin ze* chest, and most importantly, it must *compleement ze* beat. You *haf* to sense *ze* relationship between voice pulsation and *ze* score.

Breath control! Breath control! Breath control!

Ve try again! Listen to *ze* beat and try to *seenchronize* your breathing to it before *emeetting* sound."

"Yes Madam Kordovanska, I will try again."

Moksha Kordovanska, retired from grand opera before any of her students were born, was rumored to be 92 years old, but looked 81. Or was it that she was 81 years old and looked 92. It depended on whether you were wearing your bifocals or not when making the judgment.

Her heyday was centered in her place of birth, a small village near Sofia, Bulgaria. It was somewhat distant from the major opera centers of the day, and many years prior to the advent of commercial recordings in that part of the world. Her claims of stardom as a celebrated contralto were never certified in any way. However, this did not diminish her abilities as an excellent vocal coach, very much prized by the up-and-coming.

Juilliard graduate Elaine Marker was the 23-year-old second-place winner of the 2005 Metropolitan Opera's Newcomers Award and was now preparing for her first role at the Met.

At last, out of her high school chorus and no more appearances in *The Mikado* as Yum-Yum, especially not in Kokomo, Indiana.

Tony Bennett had a claim on San Francisco, CA.
Frank Sinatra had his on Hoboken, NJ.
Elaine had Kokomo, Indiana.

Born, raised and educated there, she lived the post-war, small-city life. Her family enjoyed the comforts of middle-class, mid-America. Dad, after 16 years of dedicated service and the consumption of 3,640 bottles of Amber Light, finally became chief accountant at Steiger's Brewery. Mom, as expected in any American novel about a middle-class family, was the school librarian.

What did you expect, hooker?

Elaine's two older brothers, Thomas and Gerald, had to live with the gibes of their classmates. What's in a name? "Tom and Jerry" was a hell of a lot of fun for their tormentors who were brought up on Saturday morning kid's TV.

It was pure hell for the boys.

And true to their cartoon heritage, they both eventually became lawyers, forming a joint practice (law, not marijuana) in, where else, Kokomo, Indiana.

Elaine always loved to sing.

As far back as her third birthday, when she sang "Happy Birthday to You." Unfortunately, it was usually to herself at her own party (no one else showed up, poor thing.) She may have had to face early relationship problems but at least she did have a good voice.

In her freshman year at Kokomo High, her wonderful voice, coupled with a natural stage presence, got her the leading role in Gilbert & Sullivan's *Mikado*. It was so successful that it was repeated every fall for the four years that she was there.

Elaine was Yum-Yummed up to here.

In those four years, Elaine's appearance changed from the awkward preteen to that of a lovely young woman. Her skin was soft and smooth, and her zits disappeared to find a new host on her chest. Zits to t- - s, you know what I mean.

Her braces were finally removed and her hair went from curly purple to wavy blond as her body created nascent, luscious feminine curves.

She became a true Yummy Yum.

By her senior year, Elaine no longer had to sing to herself at her birthday party. Her sweaty suitors were lined up.

Unknown to Elaine, Miss Ladd, her high school music teacher as well as director of *The Mikado,* had sent a tape of Elaine's Yum-Yum to the Juilliard School of Music in New York City.

The Juilliard admissions team was impressed enough to dispatch an alumnus residing in Indianapolis to Kokomo to see the performance. The person they had tapped was one Enrico Calzoni, a brilliant pianist who was forced by circumstances to give up a promising soloist career.

Two years earlier, there was the untimely passing of Enrico's father, who was only 56 years old, but according to the doctor, had the heart of a 90-year-old. His demise created an immediate void in the management of the family business, The Indianapolis Department Store. With 140 employees, it was too large to ignore, so the only child of the late Pietro Calzoni jumped into the driver's seat, but had to drop his keys.

Years later, he received the message about Elaine and cleared his calendar for the Friday evening performance at the Kokomo High School. Enrico sat there in total awe of that sensational voice. He could not move—or breathe. It also helped that the body producing that magnificent sound was not exactly chopped liver.

Based on Enrico's recommendation, and a subsequent face-to-face interview and audition with the Juilliard staff, Elaine was offered an absolutely unexpected and unsolicited, full four-year scholarship.

Would you believe she rejected it?

If you said yes, you are in desperate need of counseling.

Little Miss Marker had come to the big city and Juilliard five years ago, but not before a farewell, and very, very, very extended dinner with her now very, very, very good friend, Enrico.

Get the drift?

CHAPTER 4

After protracted negotiations, Enrico Calzoni sold the The Indianapolis Department Store to the Confederation of Retail Stores, the largest retailing group in the Midwest. Enrico was at last free to again pursue his life's twin beacons, music and Elaine's. She had been in the Big Apple for almost three years pursuing her musical career while his was but a distant memory.

At 39 he was still single, lean and in excellent health. He was also quite good-looking, in a Nordic way, as opposed to his heritage with its Italian stereotype. With a short blond beard, trimmed daily to a stylish six-day-old length and, damn it, a full head of curly blond hair. All of the above attributes, coupled with a hell of a lot of money from the sale, were the fuel that gave him the freedom to address his new mid-life crisis (does thirty-nine years old define mid-life?) with absolute confidence.

We should all face such a crisis.

Rico, as he was known to friends, finished his connection to Indianapolis with the sale of his Beamer and Dad's Caddy, along with both Dad's house and his own, and all of their furnishings. The only exceptions were his grand piano and those two magnificent paintings from his collection.

He was at last an absolutely free agent, with zero responsibilities or commitments. With an ear-to-ear grin frozen on his face, he boarded AA 602 from Indianapolis to LaGuardia, with a one-way ticket. The cost of the flight was cheaper than his last telephone bill, with all of the calls to Elaine in NYC. Not that either made the slightest dent in his new, significantly expanded, financial portfolio.

~~

"No, Ms. Walsh, I said that I need an apartment with a large bedroom, a very large living room/studio. This place could not even accommodate an upright, and my Steinway is a concert grand model."

"No, Ms. Walsh, the master bedroom is to comfortably sleep two adults, not one pygmy."

"No, Ms. Walsh, a bathroom en suite is a necessity."

"No, Ms. Walsh, I really do need a kitchen."

"Yes, Ms. Walsh, congratulations. By God, you did it. It's perfect! Not only does it meet my specs, and is but three blocks from Lincoln Center, but you actually kept it under $7.5 million. It's a real bargain, for Manhattan."

Using all of the contacts from his previous life in the family business, Rico gained entry to the wholesale furniture and furnishings market. The Design Center on East 45th Street was immediately accommodating upon presentation of his old business card. Within two weeks he was very comfortably ensconced in his new home 22 floors above Central Park between 73rd and 74th Streets.

There was only one unresolved problem, and it was a biggie.

~~

Now on to part two of Rico's severely limited time on this planet.

Remember, only you and I know about the first Chapter, and we are sworn to secrecy.

Rico still thinks he has a long happy life ahead of him.

CHAPTER 5

During the late 1950's, Captain Cornelius Magnus Collins had been a much-revered institution in the NYPD for some 19 years until his untimely death at the hands of a couple of "Nasties."

Actually, they were real sons of bitches.

But again, I get ahead of myself.

Cornelius had a highly-developed skill of second-sensing and then honing in on the smallest of details, which always, yes, always, led to the early resolution of even the thorniest of cases. His very competent peers would often call him in for advice and/or "Where have I gone astray?" talks. That is the esteem he had earned in his years with the department.

One really dreary Friday afternoon, Connie, as he was known by all in the Department, was called in when one of his teams hit a really major snag in negotiating the release of a hostage who had been taken during a corner convenience store robbery that had gone very wrong.

They very rarely go very "right."

The Pakistani shop owner, having been robbed three times in the last two years, had absolutely refused to open his cash register. Enough is enough!

The Donen twins callously shot him in the head, grabbed the $22.48 from the register, and ran off using his young clerk as a shield. The two of them ran two blocks with the poor kid in-between, a gun to his head.

They made it safely to their tenement hideaway on Avenue B near 9th street. The building was almost immediately surrounded by the elite NYPD fast-response team, including snipers. The latter were positioned on adjoining rooftops and in commandeered apartment windows with a view of the hideaway. Beyond that, the block between 9th and 10th streets was cordoned off and filled with every conceivable type of emergency vehicle. Blinking red and blue lights, emergency radios, uniforms of all description with drawn weapons were everywhere. Yellow tape kept the press and gawkers a block away.

The not-too-bright bad guys' position was untenable, and they knew it even without knowing the meaning of the word untenable. However, these two idiots were not about to re-start a new life in prison. After all, they had just gotten early release only two weeks ago for Good Behavior, after serving 8 years of a 15-year sentence.

They had been convicted for, guess what?

You got it. A convenience store robbery.

So much for our much-vaunted parole system.

The Donens were obviously specialists, but equally as obvious, very poorly trained for their specialty.

The brothers soon toughened their stance and shouted out a two-hour deadline. If all charges were not dropped within two hours, they would kill their hostage. They had nothing to lose as they already had a first-degree murder conviction facing them.

That was it! Take it or leave it.

A background check with their former prison warden and a prison psychiatrist produced the complex picture of two extremely unstable young men with years of psychiatric treatment, drugs, and very long rap sheets. Not a happy situation.

The call went out for Connie to join the team. He was there in twelve minutes.

After an hour, Connie managed to negotiate himself as a replacement for the young hostage. After all, he reasoned with them, wouldn't the police be more careful if their boss was in the direct line of fire?

In full view of the tenement building, Connie laid his gun on the ground, showed from the distance that he had no hidden arms, and walked into the building. As he entered their apartment, they released the teenager.

Connie tried to reason with them as he had successfully done on so many other occasions, but he was talking to two unemotional stone faces with dead eyes.

Absolutely no progress, with but five minutes remaining in the deadline, unstable hot-blood replaced lukewarm humanity. No, it is not Nature vs. Nurture.

It is No Trace.

No trace of intelligence.

No trace of compassion.

No trace of humanity.

Thirty-nine-year-old Connie was simply shot in the back of the head.

Both brothers received a similar end as they stormed out of the building.

It was at that time that two-year-old Connie Jr. became fatherless, and was to be raised by his mother and aunts and uncles in and out of the Department.

Nineteen years after being nurtured by his mother and 14 of New York's finest "fathers," Connie graduated with honors from John Jay College with a degree in Public Law, and immediately joined the NYPD. There was just no question as to what Connie's kid would do in life. It was all dictated to him in his genes.

As with every rookie, Connie spent the first two years in the Department wearing out three pairs of shoes on his street beat. After proving himself with an impressive record of twelve arrests plus two murders prevented by his skills as an officer who could relate to all sorts of street life, he earned his sergeant's stripes.

A short seven years later, Connie was awarded his first bar as a Lieutenant in the homicide division, the same age his Dad was when he received his.

Junior continued to honor his father with his own well-deserved and very distinguished career. The two generations of "Connie" in the NYPD became legendary.

It was because he was so well aware of his special status in the Department, coupled with absolutely zero progress on this latest high-profile case, now dubbed Murder at the Met, that Connie was now really Pissed Off.

Did you know that Pissed Off, like the common cold, is contagious?

It is a well-known fact that when your boss has contracted this malady, all subordinates now suffer the same symptoms.

The "Malady" goes on.

~~

The common theme bugging all in the squad room that warm September morning was that the Met Murder (so dubbed by the media) was to be resolved expeditiously, with haste, great speed, quickly and most importantly—damned fast.

Each one of Connie's squad members got that same message transmitted directly to his/her brain's processing centers at the same time. Even though a room is not wired for wi-fi, we instinctively know that e-mail, Facebook, texting and tweeting are not the only current (yes, pun intended) foundations of communication. We are all connected by direct contact coupled with not-yet-thoroughly-understood emotion and thought transmission. Bill Gates, Steve Jobs and Mark Zuckerberg were not the only ones who developed unique communication channels.

The palpable group tension was the reason for this morning's 34th Precinct's Homicide squad meeting, with all members present, Connie presiding.

The prevailing Pissed-Off atmosphere was so thick, you could almost smell it.

"Ladies and Gentlemen, I have only one thing to say. By 6:00 pm this evening, when we are all, and I repeat, all, here to reconvene in this room, you will each, without exception, contribute one new, pertinent and salient finding to the resolution of this case.

Do I make myself clear?

Do I need to repeat this instruction?

No? Go."

CHAPTER 6

"Doc, you're up first. Tell me something I had not known before 6:00 pm today."

Dr. Stephen Hochschuler, the renowned and internationally respected Medical Examiner of the City of New York, sat comfortably perched on the table's edge and said in his usual grave (yup, yet another pun intended) manner, "We finally got the lab test results I had requested last Tuesday. They required an extended processing time because of the complexity of the lab procedures.

We aspirated and swabbed the inner linings of the deceased's lungs and found some particularly interesting results.

First, there were threads, dust and mite particles that were traced back to samples taken from the red pillow on the deceased's couch. It confirms the suspected theory of imposed suffocation at his apartment as the cause of death.

Blood work revealed the second pertinent item found, traces of sodium-penta-folinate. This is a relatively rare commercial drug that is used only in hospitals to induce an immediate involuntary, but temporary, coma in patients. Our hypothesis is that the murderer first incapacitated the victim with the drug in a surprise move, and then placed the pillow over his face, causing silent death within one minute.

A very important point of this finding is that sodium-penta-folinate is a closely controlled substance that is only available in hospital dispensaries.

The FDA requires that careful dispensing records must be maintained. Additionally, there is only one manufacturer of this drug in the US, GosChem Pharmaceuticals, in Brewster NY. They, too, must maintain detailed records of production and disbursement.

Find the anomaly in the records and you may have a lead to someone with access, but not medical need."

Connie then chimed in, "Thanks Doc for our first solid investigative path."

He then continued, "Watkins and Carol, after your individual reports to this group, I want you to go over the records of all NYC and area hospitals as well as those of GosChem and see if you can find any unaccounted-for shortages. See who had access to the dispensaries, legally or not. Get together with Doc and find out exactly what to look for in terms of dosage as well as how it is handled.

Franco, you are up next."

Sergeant Francis DiAngelo was Connie's second-in-command, right-hand and alter ego. When Connie suffered from such common constraints as only 24 hours in a day, or having to be in two places at the same time, Franco became Connie redux. As his surrogate, Franco accomplished the task at hand just as Connie would have.

He was the comer in the Department and Connie was his mentor.

"I spent the day at the vic's apartment and once again went over the known facts to see where the holes were. What were we missing that was staring us right in the face?

I paced the apartment for three hours, stared at the walls, and looked behind everything that was covered and into every nook and cranny. I repeated the above actions at least 431 times.

Then I saw it! Literally saw it, right in front of me—on the wall. Remember the two mural-sized paintings in the living room, by the artist Barbara Gray?

The dates on both the "Blue Nile" and "White Nile" was 2005, some two years before the victim moved into the NY apartment. As a matter of fact they were painted around the time he met his soon-to-be fiancé. I don't believe in coincidences, and neither do you.

What had been accomplished during his last few weeks in Indiana was the sale of all of his possessions. Why not those two paintings? Then again, when were they actually bought? Beyond their absolute beauty, what was it about them that was so important to him? I pored through all of his financial records and found that he had actually acquired them prior to selling his family business, but did not take possession until just before the move.

What was the true meaning to him in these paintings? Why were they the only items, beyond clothing, that he shipped to NYC? Even family heirlooms, photos, silver, china and furniture were auctioned off before he left Indiana.

The "why" bugged me, so I had both paintings removed from the wall for a more extensive examination.

They are now at the forensics lab undergoing non-invasive testing by the in-house team, soon to be shipped for supplemental testing by experts at the Metropolitan Museum of Art. We should have a preliminary report within the next few days."

"Thanks, Franco. Stick with it until the results are in."

"Ozzie, let's hear from you".

Everyone called him Ozzie as no one around there could pronounce Ozdjemti, the name given to him in his native Sudan. His formative years were spent with his parents and two siblings during the non-ending brutal wars between the Arab north and the tribal south.

One hot late afternoon, seven-year-old Ozzie had been sent to the stream about four miles from the family hut to fetch a canister of water. When he returned some 4 ½ hours later, his home was still burning and the charred bodies of his entire family, his entire world, were scattered on the blood-soaked ground. This seven-year-old child scraped at the ground with sticks and his bare hands until the hole was deep enough to bury the few remains of his entire family. It was only after his final farewell to all he had known and loved that he made his way to the big city, Khartoum.

Ozzie's suffering was all too common in that part of the world and this child became one of the many roaming the streets with no other purpose other than to survive yet another day. He was unusually bright and used newly acquired skills of survival to create a job delivering coffee to street side vendors that netted him only pennies a day. His friendly demeanor, ready smile and work ethic soon won his obtaining the coveted job of delivering to the US Embassy staff. They fell in love with the street urchin. He was soon used for all of their personal errands.

He became such a favorite that when it was time for the Ambassador to recommend orphans for the repatriation program to the States, his name was at top of the list. Their loss became a positive gain for the USA.

Raised by sympathetic and very encouraging foster parents, an obviously naturally gifted Ozzie breezed through the NYC public school system, eventually graduating from the State University of New York (SUNY) with a degree in Industrial Psychology.

He immediately joined the Department.

It was time to help those who had helped him.

"I spent the day once again leafing through the victim's papers to see what was missed the first ten times of such perusal. There was this twitch in the back of my neck that kept telling me that I had missed something important. After six hours, there it was, staring at me, yelling, "Stupid! I tried to catch your attention some nine readings ago."

It was the deceased's name on the family-owned store's incorporation papers, along with that of a co-owner. Yes, the deceased had a partner.

CHAPTER 7

"No, that one won't do. I need a carrying case with sturdy wheels for my contrabass. I can't schlep this humongous bass superstrings to concerts, auditions and rehearsal halls in a case with microscopic tin wheels that will fail at a most inconvenient time."

The helpful clerk walked him to the other side of the shop and said, "This one is slightly more expensive, sir, but has reinforced rubber tread wheels 5" in diameter. Even though it is used and has experienced some superficial scratches, it is still solid, has like-new velveteen lining, is well balanced, and the price is right."

The customer raised his horn-rimmed glasses, scratched his scraggly red beard, encircled the case twice and measured the inside three times to ensure fit, before committing himself.

"OK, I'll take it. No need to gift-wrap it. It's not my birthday and I know I'm getting it."

His lame attempt to lighten the conversation did not lead to the hoped-for additional price reduction, so he just peeled off the well-used bills from his money clip, paid the clerk, and rolled his new old case out the back door to the parking lot.

The pearl-gray Lexus RX 350 SUV was parked about 20 feet away in an alleyway. Using his remote, he raised the rear cargo door and stowed the case. With the rear seatbacks lowered before he had left his home, it fit perfectly.

As he pulled out of the alleyway, Charlie Mallard removed his glasses so that he could actually see what he was doing and where he was going. The itchy red beard came off next, followed by the crumpled old jacket and hat, complete with matted red hair strewn under it, which he had donned to complete the deception. It had to come off before he could drive to his next destination. This was a precaution in the unlikely event that he was stopped for a traffic infraction. There was no use taking unnecessary chances at this point, the mark of the professional that he was. As a matter of fact the only thing he retained at this point was the name Charlie Mallard. Not his own, of course, but a convenient one used from time to time.

It was the 16 years of training, executing and perfecting in his previous profession as a Black Operations covert agent for the CIA that provided the expertise he had developed to cover his true persona as well as his tracks.

It all really began at Camp Perry, the CIA training facility near Williamsburg, Virginia, popularly referred to as the "The Farm" where he (whatever his name was then) learned the tradecraft.

Later, field experience in the USSR, Bulgaria and Rumania during the Bad Old Days of the Cold War had given him the opportunity to perfect the things he had recently learned, and subsequently guided him through the remainder of whatever was the task at hand.

After a dozen or so years of fun work, but at peon wages, it was time for him to move on, and so he did, as a private contractor.

Just because the government was no longer his employer did not mean his life, as he had lived it, had to end. After all, at this stage of his life he couldn't suddenly become a brain surgeon.

All three parts of the execution of this execution contractually had to be featured in bold headlines that would reach the international news media. A very unusual and newsworthy public arena was the only way that Charlie's overseas "sponsor" would be able to read about the deed and the identity of the deceased.

Said confirmation would then trigger payment for his services rendered.

Thus began a very convoluted approach to what should be a simple murder. However, an extremely complicated and visible murder was now requisite in order for him to receive a very substantial bonus.

Part A had been, as expected, completed without a hitch.

However, it was already 2:20, some 20 minutes behind his well-planned schedule. As with most operations of this type, timing is absolutely critical. He now had to make up for the lost time without becoming careless.

Careless was not an option, it was a death sentence. His!

Now on to Part B.

Charlie drove to the Central Park West address given to him, and found that the building's underground garage was unattended during daylight hours, just as he had noted on previous drive-by's. Before driving in, he got out of the car and pretended to adjust his license plate. He was in reality covering it with a seemingly clear plastic sheet that rendered the numbers unreadable to a camera.

He found a remote parking spot in the building's garage, checked to ensure that the security camera was not aimed in his direction, and carefully replaced his disguise. He was now once again with beard and wig as "Eric the Red." A glance in the side rearview mirror satisfied him that he was alone. He got out of the car, retrieved his bass case, and took the garage elevator to the lobby.

A uniformed concierge immediately intercepted him and said, "Can I help you sir?"

"Yes, my name is Reynolds and I have an appointment with Professor Calzoni."

The concierge picked up the intercom, dialed 2201, waited a moment, and said, "Sir, Mr. Reynolds is here to see you. Immediately, sir!

"Mr. Reynolds, you may take the elevator on the left to the 22nd floor, and turn left to Apartment 22A."

Charlie was now only nine minutes behind schedule as the elevator door opened on the 22nd floor. He turned left to see what could only be Mr. Calzoni waiting for him at his open door.

"Mr. Reynolds, my name is Rico Calzoni. Please come in and tell me what this is all about. The call I got from our mutual friend in Indianapolis asking me to receive you was far from explicit. As a matter of fact, I don't have the vaguest idea as to who you are and why you want to see me."

"I will explain all in great detail, but first, may I use your bathroom to relieve my too-full bladder?"

"Through the door on your left."

Charlie closed the bathroom door behind him, reached into his right jacket pocket, and pulled out a handkerchief wrapped around a small plastic bottle. He carefully poured some of the liquid onto the handkerchief, at arm's length, to avoid inhaling any of the aromatic material on it, and then palmed it in his left hand.

Charlie flushed the toilet, opened the door, and re-entered the living room.

"Now Mr. Reynolds, what is all this urgency that was intimated to me on the phone this morning?"

"It goes back to . . . wait a sec, is that a fire in the building on the next block? See the thick black smoke?"

Rico looked out the window in the direction pointed out. He started to ask which one, when a hand clasping a cloth with a pungent smell covered his nose and mouth. He slumped to the floor without even finishing the last sentence he was ever to utter.

Without missing a beat, Charlie grabbed a pillow from the sofa and covered Rico's face until both breathing and pulse stopped.

It was as fast as that.

Better still, a quick look at his plain vanilla watch showed that he had even regained the lost 9 minutes.

Try to never deviate from the plan.

After wiping all surfaces that he had touched and restoring the room to its former pristine condition, Charlie positioned Rico's body in a sitting stance, within the double-bass case. The pungent handkerchief was then placed in a small plastic bag, sealed and placed in his pocket. Using a second handkerchief, he closed the door behind him and pushed the elevator call button with his knuckle. He did the same in the elevator, remembering first to also wipe clean the 22nd floor button.

As he wheeled his case from the apartment floor elevator to the one that served the garage, he smiled and politely nodded thanks to the concierge.

Now around the corner to the garage elevator, and out of the concierge's view, he covered the call button with his extra handkerchief and once again as he pushed the G button in the elevator.

One long click on his remote opened the Lexus tailgate as he approached the car. He hefted the heavy case in, closed the door and walked around to the driver's door.

Still not a soul in the garage.

After he drove past the range of the external security camera, he pulled to the side and jumped out to pull off the plastic sheet that had obscured his license plate numbers. Charlie once again removed his uncomfortable beard, glasses, etc.

Now onto the real fun part, Part C.

CHAPTER 8

Her shoes came off first, each kicked to a different corner of the room. Her coat flew off next and onto the couch as she punched the button on the answering machine. While waiting for the day's messages, Elaine opened the fridge, pulled out the lone bottle on the door shelf where the milk should have been, and poured a rejuvenating glass of Santa Margherita Pinot Grigio white wine.

The staccato voice intoned, "You have one new message. Push 1 to listen."

"Hi, sweetie, this is Rico. It's furnished, heated and filled to the brim with: Lox, wine-Stock and "Crate and Barrel." It's all here and it's mine, soon to be ours and you have to be the first to see it. The seductive aroma of my secret recipe lasagna will overwhelm your senses, which is in the oven as I speak. The lasagna that is, not my senses. My twin secrets of seduction never fail to tease both of your palettes. The '92 Chateau Belleville is not just breathing, it's panting on the table. Balducci's country paté, the second best spread I have ever experienced, awaits you. There is also the "Can't Wait" me. Please don't tell me you have previous plans! Use my new home phone number as it was finally connected yesterday."

The answering machine time stamp clocked the call in at 10:30 that morning.

The voice, his message, brought back the memory of their first weekend away together, a euphemism for "You know what." She saw it in full color on the giant HD screen of her mind.

We drove Northeast for about three hours to the Gateway Inn, a rustic family-owned and run Connecticut B&B, with only five guest rooms. It was justifiably renowned for its memorable breakfasts and dinners. The four-poster beds, surrounded by authentic period furnishings, completed the idyllic picture book bedroom where the real dessert was to be served.

I was never to forget any detail of the next three hours.

Without a spoken word, we simultaneously kicked off our shoes and approached each other for a prolonged embrace. No words, no kissing, no fondling, just an embrace. It seemed to last for, and certainly felt like, 12 ½ years of floating in soft clouds.

As we broke that magnetic bond, Enrico said, "It's time to become religious, something I am not particularly noted for.

We are about to experience an almost biblical 'Enrico's Fourteen Stations of De-Frost.'

It was not until we had both shed our clothes and inhibitions that I began to understand and experience what had been said.

As I lay on the bed with my eyes open in warm anticipation, he bent over me and gently kissed them closed, murmuring, "That's one."

I felt his lips move to the sides of my neck, just under my ears as he intoned, "That's two." A soft purr found its own involuntary way from my soul to my mouth. I heard the barely audible numbers three and four as lips gently caressed each breast. The number five was partially lost in the softness of my belly.

Six and seven were only just heard as I felt sensations in my left inner thigh and my left calf. The purring became louder and absolutely uncontrollable!

Eight was noted on my left ankle, followed by nine at my left big toe. The not-so-soft purring was now accompanied by tensing, warming and uncontrollable movement of my entire body.

My right big toe earned the number ten, followed by eleven and twelve at my right ankle and calf. The purring transformed into a soft moaning. I had no idea where this was coming from. I had no control over any of my feelings or reactions. They were just there.

Thirteen was whispered when lips caressed my right inner thigh. My legs gently parted allowing fourteen to be kissed, explored and penetrated creating the necessary conditions for flight.

Forget the nonsense about seven minutes. I exploded immediately as powerful thrust was established."

"JERUSALEM, WE HAVE LIFT-OFF!"

Back to the real world, it was now only 4:30.
"Whoa, where is my left pearl earring? Elaine asked in vain as she got out of bed. You know the ones. You gave them to me just last week. I had both on when we were at the first Station and now it is missing. If I weren't so squeamish I would have had my ear pierced years ago. Now this is the price I have to pay. It just popped into my head that you and Vermeer, the old Dutch artist, are co-creators of "The Girl With One Pearl Earring."
After looking under the bed and other furniture in the room, she

finally found the errant earring hidden under a crumpled blanket. Her left lobe once again regained its prize. That is, until her smooth earlobes once again would allow another deviant adornment to slip away.

Elaine decided that there was enough time to draw her bath and excise the day, before returning Rico's call. A half-hour soak coupled with some voice exercises was absolutely called for.

That glorious voice echoing off the tiles in the closed 6'x10' room, issuing forth from that naked goddess was what Rico lived for. Both of his loves fulfilled in a tiny room.

At 5:10, Elaine toweled off and began those feminine primordial processes of selecting "what to wear," followed by her natural beauty's unnecessary "war paint."

After selecting the beige cashmere sweater, brown slacks and brown pumps (Rico's abbreviated height precluded high heels), Elaine picked up the phone.

Twelve rings before answering is not unusual in England. In the States it definitely means, "I'm not here." Obviously, the requisite telephone answering machine had not yet been hooked up.

"Oh well," she murmured to herself. He must have stepped out at the last minute for the forgotten baguette—or maybe for an answering machine. She'd try again after the very feminine ritual of putting on her "face."

Thirty minutes later, sixteen rings produced the same results.

It was already 6:00 PM and she was expected, so there was only one thing to do. Go.

Elaine's co-op building was adequate and of pre-war vintage, with some wonderful touches not found in the more modern buildings. One such item was the "Taxi Call" button in the elevator. By the time she reached the lobby, the doorman had a cab waiting for her.

"422 Central Park West, please."

Why did she have this nagging feeling in the pit of her stomach? After all, he had only stepped out for a baguette, or an answering machine. Why the panic?

At 6:25, Elaine entered the uncluttered white and lime marble lobby of 422 and presented herself to the doorman.

"Sorry Ma'am, Mr. Calzoni does not seem to be at home."

"No, Ma'am, I have not spoken to him since that gentleman came for his contra bass lesson. I did not know that Mr. Calzoni was such a gifted musician and teacher."

"What contra bass lesson? Rico is a pianist."

"Would you be Ms Elaine Marker, ma'am?"

"Yes, how do you know my name?"

"When Mr. Calzoni moved in last week he left an extra key with me for your convenience. It's in my locked cabinet. Just a moment.

"Ah, here it is Ms Marker, and as per his instructions you are free to use it at any time. My name is Geraldo, and I am here five days a week. My colleagues and I are at your service 24/7."

"Thank you, Geraldo. What apartment is he in, when he is in?"

"22A, ma'am, and welcome."

The heavy bronze elevator door opened on the 22nd floor revealing a small but smartly furnished lobby with a door at each end, 22A and 22B. She turned left to 22A and rang the bell just to make sure the concierge was right about Rico being out for the moment.

No response, so she used the key.

While looking for the light switch the enticing aroma of what could only be Rico's familiar and absolutely fabulous lasagna came wafting to the door.

That elicited smile number 1.

Smile number 2 came when she turned on the lights revealing a small reception area with a clear glass-topped pedestal table directly in front of her. The table groaned under the weight of a magnificent vase of huge red and yellow gladiola. The variegated tentacles of a Chihuly glass chandelier suspended just above echoed their colors.

Momentary suspended animation followed.

When she came back from her Technicolor high, she called out, "Rico."

Still no answer.

The exploration continued as Elaine stepped down the two steps into the sunken living room. It almost felt like three steps as she plunged into the deep, plush white carpet. The carpet was so deep that it even retained the twin wheel impressions that the mover's dolly must have left.

There was a wall of windows at the far end of the room overlooking Central Park. Each one framed a master painting done by Mrs. Nature.

They were beautifully complemented by the two mural-sized abstract paintings on either side of the room. "The White Nile" on her left whispered to the "The Blue Nile" on her right. Rico had bought both some time ago when he said he had met the famed artist, Barbara Gray, at her Chelsea gallery.

There was a brown leather sofa under "The White Nile" and two plush chairs upholstered in orange velvet under "The Blue Nile." An off-white, square stone table separated the chairs, complementing the stone mosaic coffee table in front of the sofa. Of course, Rico's beloved Steinway sat in front of the windows. In-ceiling spots were strategically placed to illuminate his keyboard, the paintings and his favored reading sites.

Rico's taste had always been impeccable.

To the right of "The Blue Nile" were flush solid twin oak doors leading into the formal dining room. Rico had selected a classic Danish-modern oval teak table with 6 matching high backed chairs. The sideboard was an old, very heavy, English oak country cupboard. They were made for each other, some 200 years apart! The still life with dead edible things lying on a table, hung over it, completing the setting. The artist, like his models, had been dead for about 300 years and was still unknown.

There was a small door on the right leading to the powder room. Just opposite her was a swinging door, she guessed correctly, leading to the kitchen. This was not really a guess as the aroma of Rico's lasagna came wafting through the door. There was also the constant pinging sound coming from the oven control panel. The lasagna apparently had been baked using the automatic timer, which was telling all within earshot that "I'm finished, and have turned myself off."

The kitchen was as she had imagined, a chef's delight, as Rico had the self-taught qualifications of a true chef. Even if the lasagna was lousy, and it most certainly never was, the aroma alone was a testament to these qualifications.

Strange, she thought. Rico never left dirty dishes around. Even when in the midst of preparation, he cleaned as he cooked. As she always left piles of dishes and utensils to the very end of the day, this was a frequent theme of their good-natured "foreplay."

He must have really forgotten some important ingredient to run out like that, and leave such a mess. When he gets back he will not hear the end of my teasing! It might even lead into "five-play."

Back through the dining room, past the "Blue Nile," and through the door next to the "White Nile" which led into his bedroom suite.

The only surprise here was the pair of cooking trousers he had strewn on the king-sized bed. Obviously, he hadn't even had the time to toss it in the hamper before running out on his errand.

Mister Fastidious had goofed again.

More fodder for the now "five-play" fire! Who knows, we might even get to a record setting "six-play."

Elaine went back into the living room, kicked off her shoes, picked up a copy of *Opera News* lying on the coffee table, and stretched out on the leather sofa.

It wasn't until the third ring that Elaine shook off the grogginess of the deep sleep she had obviously fallen into, and found the house phone.

"Hi, sweetie, where are you?" she playfully questioned.

"Excuse me, Ms Marker, this is the concierge, Geraldo. There are some gentlemen from the police department who are now on their way up to Mr. Rico's apartment. I checked their ID's, but they would not state their business."

"Thank you, Geraldo."

Not more than 30 seconds later the doorbell rang.

CHAPTER 9

Elaine took one look at the picture and slumped to the floor. The officers helped her to the couch and brought her some water. Shock was soon replaced with a quickened heartbeat and dazed disbelief.

Finally, her mind accepted the reality of what was being presented to her.

"Yes, that's my Rico!" With sudden realization, she changed it to "That was my Rico."

What happened?

When?

Why?

How?

Do you know who did this?

Where is Rico now?

"Ma'am, we know this comes as a horrible shock and will try to answer as many of your questions as we can, but first, would you like some more water?"

"No, thank you, please just tell me what you know."

Detectives Bailey and Watkins sat down so that Ms Marker would not have to look up at them. Their many years of combined experience taught them about the fear induced by looming authority figures. This woman, not yet a suspect, did not need fear introduced at this point.

Edward Gray

After telling Elaine about the known circumstances of Mr. Calzoni's death, they proceeded to question her.

"I left my apartment at 10:15 this morning for an 11:00 am doctor's appointment. Yes, it was Dr. Feinberg, my ENT specialist, who tends to any throat irritations before they have an effect on my voice. He has his office on the corner of 59th Street and Sixth Avenue.

I walked from there to Balboa's to have lunch with two friends.

That's correct, the one on 49th Street. We were there from noon to about 2:00 pm. I then walked directly to Madame Kordovanska for my 2:30, 1½ hour voice lesson. I believe I got home about 4:30 pm."

She continued, in response to Detective Maleski's question, "I last saw Rico for dinner, two nights ago. We met at Rosa Mexicana, off Broadway near Lincoln Center at 6:00 pm before going to the opera at 8:00 pm. Yes, I do, detective. It was *Turandot* that evening. Afterwards, because Rico expected the last of his furniture deliveries early the next morning, we both felt it to be prudent for his taxi to drop me off at my building. It was just before midnight."

Watkins diligently recorded her statement, filling in names and addresses for later confirmation.

They showed Elaine their court order and asked her for permission to check the apartment. Still slumped on the couch, and with all energy completely sapped, Elaine silently nodded her approval.

They slipped on their latex gloves for a preliminary check while confirming to her the need for the police forensics squad to "fine comb" the apartment for anything that could shed light on Mr. Calzoni's murder.

After a cursory once-over of the apartment, they located boxes of papers mostly in packing cases, obviously still from the move. They checked drawers, closets and the piano bench for any additional papers. These would be brought to the station for detailed examination. One never knew where a paper trail might lead.

Having received notification when the alarm first went out and an address confirmed, the forensics team had immediately mobilized and sped to the apartment. They arrived within twenty minutes of the two detectives and immediately took pictures of the entire apartment. This was followed by their usual, almost microscopic, examination of all surfaces, furniture, clothing, papers, toiletries, etc. A set of Elaine's fingerprints was taken before dusting for alien prints. Fingerprints would probably prove to be not terribly helpful as decorating and moving crews had been all over the place during the last few weeks.

"Watkins, speak to the concierge and get his delivery and visitor logs going back to when Mr. Calzoni first took possession of the apartment. Then locate each individual who was here, take statements and get prints for forensics comparison.

"Ms Marker, I apologize for asking this of you, but would you be so kind as to accompany us to the Medical Examiner's Office as we need an official identification before he can begin the autopsy."

CHAPTER 10

Master Bagel Baker Nina Ruelle had learned the disappearing skill of preparing authentic New York bagels from her grandfather, who in turn had learned it from his, etc. The family secrets went back at least four generations to the small bakery in Bucharest that had initially developed the recipe. A specific mix of available flours, secrets of seasoning, amount of and when to add water, kneading method and time, resting of dough, immersion in boiling water time, baking temperatures, type of oven and baking time, cooling time and finishing operations were all family secrets.

No other bagel bakery in New York, or the rest of the States for that matter, had mastered all of these steps.

Additionally, Nina had one distinct advantage over her own forbears as well as the rest of the US: New York City water! Its distinct characteristics, primarily a very low calcium content, insured that special bouquet to the bagels that made Sam's Bagels the yardstick against which all others were measured.

Nina happily carried on this family tradition, but at the same high personal cost that was experienced by all of her predecessors. The bakery consumed almost all of her waking hours. Six days a week her alarm went off at 2:30 am. She showered, dressed, donned her blue helmet, got on her matching Harley and after a 22-minute drive, parked it in the alley at Sam's back door.

After unlocking the bagelry door she turned off the alarm and turned on the kitchen lights. Her helmet, with keys always placed dangling on the chin strap, avoided her yelling at 6:00 pm, the end of her workday, "Has anyone seen my keys?"

Nina's daily gift to the city was about to begin.

⁂

One of the very few routines that Charlie Mallard had tried so hard to break (because it became so routine), but absolutely could not resist, was that when in New York he had to go at least once to the fabled Sam's Bagelry on Second Avenue and 54th Street for breakfast.

Of course, when doing so all of his mental defenses were on high alert. He had to fit in, so it was extremely important for him to learn the local lingo in order to properly order the house specialty—without calling attention to himself.

"Gimmee a burnt scooped garbage with a shmear, novy and a slice. Also a cuppa black."

Translation for the uninitiated is:

"Please kind sir, may I have a toasted bagel coated with various seeds, onion and garlic chips, with the insides scooped and discarded. Both denuded halves are to be placed side by side on a plate. They are each to be slathered with a quarter inch thick coating of Philadelphia Cream Cheese, a mound of Nova Scotia smoked salmon and an eighth inch thick slice of raw onion. I would also very much like to have an accompaniment of a cup of regular coffee, that is, without the unnecessary dilution of cream, sugar or any other distractive flavoring.

Thank you, kind sir."

That made him appear to be a regular customer, thus basically invisible.

Or so he thought.

Eight days after he had completed his chosen work assignment and but a few days before his planned departure for parts only known to himself, Charlie was determined to reward himself with his usual New York feast.

He took the short walk from his hotel to Sam's, where once through the front door the aroma rush alone was enough to reinvigorate his spirit. It was even enough to break through his cultivated resistance to such habitual behavior.

"After all, I don't need much but don't I occasionally deserve some form of enjoyment after a successful mission?" was his inner rationale.

"Gimmee..." etc.

Jaimie Rivera was next in line patiently waiting his turn when he heard, and immediately recognized the voice in front of him. His eyes moved up and saw large shoulders of the same shape as the ones that wheeled that big bass case into his lobby.

There was no doubt in his mind. Except for the lack of a red beard this was the same guy that had asked for Mr. Calzoni, when he was on duty as concierge that awful morning.

He immediately yelled to Stan, behind the counter, "I'm late, so will be back later for my morning fix," and went outside.

He ran across the street, to the entrance of the adjoining Trader Joe's, and immediately dialed 911.

After but one ring, a female voice asked "What is your emergency?"

"My name is Jaimie Rivera and I am the day concierge at 882 Fifth Avenue. I just saw the man that I believe the police are looking for in the murder of Mr. Calzoni. He is at Sam's Bagelry on Second Avenue. I can still see him through the window. He does not have that red beard, but I immediately knew who he was. It is that bastard!"

"Yes sir, please stay on the line as I forward the information for immediate action."

Charlie's many years in the business continuously honed all of the senses. That is an absolute imperative, otherwise you don't last anywhere near the 20-odd years he had been at it.

Without a backward glance, Charlie immediately processed the sudden departure of someone behind him. That was more than enough info to fire up his internal survival instincts.

While the clerk was involved in wrapping up his bagel order, Charlie excused himself saying to Stan, "Be back in a sec" and casually walked toward the men's room. Instead of turning right he took an immediate left to the kitchen swinging door.

He slipped in without a sound, immediately behind the young woman who was totally absorbed in the task of removing bagels-to-be from the vat of boiling water. Her ear buds filled her auditory senses with her chosen "boiling water music" (definitely not Handl's "Water Music" Suite) that she loved and played while involved in this specific chore, completely masking any noise Charlie may have inadvertently made.

He made none.

Nina was in her own busy world and other than her chore at hand, was completely oblivious to her surroundings

Spotting the biker's blue helmet on the wall to his left, Charlie silently lifted it off the hook, and pocketed the dangling keys. He donned the helmet as he slipped out the back door. There were two bikes, however the blue one was a Harley, and certainly matched the helmet's color. The finely tuned bike caught on the first press of the start button, just as the sound of approaching, but still blocks away, police sirens began to fill the air.

The noise of the bagel press masked the noise of the Harley startup and departure. Poor Nina had no idea that her precious bike had just been hijacked by the most hunted person in the world.

Quite different from her usual day at the bagelry.

Charlie, using his survival instincts, headed in the direction of the approaching police. Within 30 seconds he passed an oncoming stream of black and whites with screaming sirens.

He spotted an alley up ahead on the right and zoomed in and parked the bike behind an overfilled dumpster that was ripe for collection. The helmet was tossed into the dumpster, along with his parka and cap.

Charlie smoothed his hair straight back and donned heavy frame plain glass eyeglasses (always with him for just such an emergency.)

A different man from the one that had just ridden in now emerged from the alleyway into the stream of pedestrians on Third Avenue.

His survival mode was now in overdrive and seeking an appropriate opportunity to live yet another day.

The authorities had his profile and knew him to be an absolute loner. They would soon be looking for a male with certain physical characteristics (tall and well built), on his own, and obviously dangerous. He was last seen wearing a black parka and cap.

Charlie had bought some additional time by heading in the direction of the police sirens. The first place they would start looking for him would be the area away from their approach. That gave him precious minutes.

He also was aware that it would be just a matter of another few minutes before the area he was now in would be swarming with NYC police and be reinforced a short time later by federal agents.

He knew that the entire area would soon be cordoned off, with all males inside the boxed off area fitting his description to be targeted for intensive interrogation.

A merry-go-round of ideas circled his mind. He immediately threw out options for a complete change in identity as the necessary items were obviously not available to him.

This left just two options. The first was to find a nearby place to hide. This idea was rejected as there would certainly be a thorough search of the area, building by building, room by room, closet by closet.

The remaining thought still circling his mind was the use of others to help change his identity. They probably would not target groups or obvious locals.

A loner does not have "others!"

Serendipity is never at one's beck and call. However, it seems to have served Charlie well on an as-needed basis on so many occasions, and there was one such potential about 20 feet ahead on Charlie's right.

Just outside of Flo's Baby Accessories shop was a parked baby carriage with no one in sight.

CHAPTER 11

Beth Jameson, mother of four-month-old Kenneth, was on her way to meet the JULIETS (Justly United Lively Intelligent Individual Entertaining Trendy Sisters) for their weekly breakfast at Sam's Bagelry. It was on the block before when little Kenneth decided to give up his earlier breakfast, onto his very new blanket.

No way to clean up the really smelly mess and no way could she bring same into Sam's.

That's when she passed good old Flo's, her go-to store for most of Kenneth's needs.

Beth thought about it and concluded, "The carriage will not fit through the door. I can just leave Ken in his carriage out front, in the sun, for the five minutes that it will take to buy a new blanket."

As she popped into Flo's, Charlie caught sight of a carriage named serendipity.

He slipped behind the carriage and casually pushed it in the assumed role of the harried father. On the very next block he was stopped by the quickly established cordon of police officers checking all leaving the area.

The officer in front of him looked at the stooped-over harried father with a hangdog expression pushing the carriage with a smelly infant and as a recent dad himself, knew what the poor guy was going through.

He said with an understanding smile, "Go through, sir, and get that kid changed."

Charlie pushed on for two more blocks and stopped at the main entrance to Bloomingdales.

He said to the doorman, "I have my son in a very unpleasant situation. I need to go inside to find his mother, but can't take this bundle of smell inside. Here's a tenner! Can you just keep an eye on him for the few minutes it will take for me to find her and get back here?"

"Certainly, sir."

Charlie hurried to the men's department on the ground floor and immediately picked out a bright blue blazer as well as a black zip-up jacket. He told the clerk that he would take the blazer but not the jacket. The jacket was put on the side. He then used cash to pay for the blazer. While the clerk was distracted in double-checking the sales code Charlie stuffed his own jacket <u>and</u> the new black one under it, into the store bag.

He said, "I think I will wear the new one," and donned it.

He found his way to the men's restroom and went into a stall where he again changed, this time into the black zip-up. His own jacket and the new blue blazer were then stuffed well into the bottom of a trash container.

Charlie exited Bloomingdale's at one of the other side entrances. He walked one block north and boarded the crosstown bus, through Central Park, to the west side.

His West Side Bank was his first destination. There he gained entry to one of his safe deposit boxes distributed in several banks throughout the city.

A major cash infusion and an ID wallet complete with driver's license, insurance cards, passport and matching credit cards now provided him with a new persona.

To complete the transition, Charlie stopped off at a trusted contact's specialty shop where he bought an overnight case, several suits, shirts, ties, etc., along with hair dye and the necessary cosmetics to change his appearance so as to match his new passport and other ID.

As in the past, he paid major dollars, in cash, to ensure no breach in this important link to his wellbeing.

An hour later, a well-dressed Mssr. Pierre Delevalle of Paris checked into the J.W. Marriott Hotel on Broadway for a six-night stay.

Hide in plain sight.

Chapter 12

"Frank Reynolds," née Charlie Mallard, née something else, pulled his van into the underground area at the Metropolitan Opera House reserved for "Artists and Staff Parking." He then repeated the same ritual of donning his wig and specs, exactly as he had rehearsed doing in his prior two reconnoitering trips.

He dragged his big bass case to the artists' entrance, smiled at the security guard on duty and while fumbling with his case, flashed his "Artist ID." With close to 500 people using this door every day it was impossible for the rotating duty officer to personally know everyone passing through or even notice if the ID was a real one. This one was a good forgery.

A really good one.

Frank was once again waved through.

The heavy case echoed through empty corridors and down two sets of ramps. He turned right, through the narrow corridor that dead-ended in the maintenance shop a level below ground. Because of the peculiar work schedules imposed on performance days, as he had carefully checked in prior visits, it too was empty.

If an evening performance is scheduled, the day crew does not arrive until three. This was a cost saving plan introduced by management in order to have the individual shift crews available before, during and after the performance without resorting to expensive overtime.

"Frank" selected a pair of faded blue coveralls from the assortment hanging on a row of wall pegs, donned it and continued with Part C.

He placed his big bass case on its back on the floor next to a double-tiered portable tool cart. He then carefully opened it and pulled Rico's body out, placed it on the cart's bottom shelf and draped it with a nearby drop cloth. Tools had been already strewn about on its top shelf.

He wheeled the cart up the ramp to the orchestra level and parked it just inside the side door leading from backstage right to the seats.

"Frank" then turned around and sprinted up one additional flight of stairs to stage left where the electrician's alcove complete with his chandelier controls was located. The large black button in the center was clearly marked "Central Sputnik." He depressed it until the massive chandelier was lowered to a marked point on the dial that indicated that it was now at seat level. This flexibility was designed into the system so that bulbs could be changed and crystals cleaned.

He then made his way through the backstage maze to the fire control room, adjacent to the Stage Manager's office. The room was exactly as he remembered it to be from his reconnoitering visits two and three days ago.

Three panels at eye level were mounted on the front wall, with pinpoint lights to designate areas where smoke had been detected. There were two circuit boards on the sloped desk in front of the panels with a myriad of test switches and alarm controls. The entire panel and alarm system was mimicked at several other points, including the Manager's office, the security center and the headquarters of the 32nd fire brigade three-quarters of a mile away.

Without a moment's hesitation, "Frank" located the test switch/alarm for the emergency generator room at the furthest corner of the lowest level. When activated, it would call all available emergency and security resources to the designated area. All others would immediately evacuate the building. This would give him the time he needed, unobserved, to complete Phase C.

A deep breath and click.

The alarm went off at all designated points while a general evacuation siren sounded throughout the building.

"Frank" ran back to the cart and wheeled it, with its heavy load, into a now empty auditorium, up the central aisle to Row K. He raced to seat K126, reached under the coveralls to his pocket for the seat ticket he had bought for cash some two weeks earlier. Satisfied that it was the right seat, he glanced up to reconfirm that 126 was dead (an appropriate seat) center under the chandelier.

He did a quick check of the hall to see if there was any movement. Good, all was quiet.

He once again reached into his pocket, this time extracting the coil of 200-pound nylon fishing line placed there earlier. Stretching up he looped one end of the line around the thick central vertical shaft of the chandelier. After tying a secure Boy Scout square knot, he tugged on it to make sure it would hold.

"Frank" went back to the cart, dragged the drop cloth along the floor, with its heavy load, to seat K126.

Another glance around revealed no prying eyes. He unwrapped his cargo, lifted the body onto the seat, placed it in a sitting position and looped the other end of the pre-measured line around Rico's neck, tying another Boy Scout square knot. Once again, he tested it to make sure it was secure.

"Frank" raced back to the cart, wheeled it through the stage right door, and left it there for the two-and-one-half minutes it took him to get back to the chandelier control panel and push the button that would once again raise the central chandelier to its previous height. The pre-measured line was now taut.

So was Rico, now seated in an upright position.

"Frank" raced back to recover the cart and returned it, along with the coveralls, to the shop.

He sped his now lighter bass case to the musician's rehearsal hall.

Exactly 2 ½ minutes, as planned.

All potential witnesses were standing about two floors below in the emergency generator room trying to figure out what the emergency was all about.

"Frank"'s double bass was still propped up in the corner, right where he had left it on the last visit, in a canvas cover. He stripped the cover off, carefully folded it, and stuffed it in the accessories compartment of his new hard case. He placed the bass in the case, closed it, set it back in the corner with a multitude of other instruments, and left the building.

Edward Gray

Part C completed exactly as planned.
A musician's timing is essential to his talent(s).
CIA experience is also helpful.
Boy Scout knot training doesn't hurt either.

CHAPTER 13

Until his 14th birthday, on July 12, 1939, Pietro Calzoni led the lonely life of a farmer's son. Other than for school, he rarely ventured off the 4.72-hectare property near the geographical center of Sicily that had defined his family's universe for at least four hundred years.

He attended school for 8 hours a day, 7 months of each year, and was out in the fields with Papa the rest of the time. On his 14th birthday, school was no longer compulsory, and was replaced by the unending rituals of plowing, seeding, tending and reaping.

That would be in the good years.

When the spring rains decided to skip Papa Sandro's little section of planet Earth, or the mule died, or the Gods decided to freeze his seedlings, or any combination of HIS revenge (for what?) on HIS humble servants, the family would have to scavenge, just to exist.

It was only on one of those rare days when the rains flooded the fields, preventing field work, and Papa was off to buy seed, that Pietro had the rare opportunity to actually play with a group of school friends.

Life was obviously not easy for the family, so Papa Sandro conferred with Mama and decided that their only child, Pietro, deserved a better life than the many generations of Calzonis had been barely able to eke out of this poor farm. Especially because of the extraordinary events that had brought their beloved Pietro into their otherwise childless life.

On Pietro's 14th birthday, Papa Sandro hitched his only mule to his only cart and prodded him to pull the cart the furthest distance it had ever ventured, 17 kilometers, to the village of Corezzio del Marno.

Corezzio was a mid-sized town on the river Salso. Some 6,700 people, probably all related to each other, considered this to be the epicenter of the world. Sandro knew it and the townspeople reasonably well, as he ventured to the mill in town at least twice a year, to sell his grain.

So it was to the mill he now went, not for the first time with an empty cart.

This time it was to see his old friend, the miller, Guido. Like Sandro, Guido's forebears had run this same mill, with the same grindstone, for countless centuries. He and Sandro had the same symbiotic personal and business relationship that had made life more pleasant and occasionally profitable.

"Ah, Sandro, what brings you here this time of year?"

"I need some advice, old friend. I need to speak to someone who can arrange for a better life for young Pietro. As we both know, it is forbidden for me to approach him directly."

"Then we must both be talking about Don Corezzo. I will bring you to him immediately."

Papa Sandro tied his ancient mule to a post and saw to water and feed for the tired animal. He and the miller walked for about nine minutes to the west side of town, far from the noise of the commercial center, and farther from the smells of the stables, farriers and mills in the east.

The large house on the hill belonged to the most important man in the entire area. It was not the Manse for the Bishop, nor was it the Mayor's lodge. As you might have guessed it belonged to Don Corezzo, for whose great-great-great grandfather the town and he were named. His esteemed great-great grandfather was given this small piece of Italia, comprising land along the Salso River for five miles in each direction, in perpetuity, by King Victor Emanuel I, for Special Services rendered.

What are a few mini-massacres among friends?

That's one important guy, and boy, did you listen to him.

Very, very carefully!

Again, as you might have guessed, the then-current Don owned most of the east side of town, the Church and most of the commercial center. What he didn't own, he still derived "income" from.

As you might have once again guessed, the latter source of income occasionally required a little "persuasion."

The "persuasion" team was a well-organized group of sub-species, who reported directly to the Don's Consigliere. The respect they commanded was directly proportional to their height, weight, swagger, musculature, black eyes, grooved faces and most importantly their well-known total dedication to the Don. He ruled their lives as well as that of the Church, the townspeople, the area's industry, surrounding hamlets and farms. His wife was the sole exception. She-who-must-be-obeyed ruled the Don.

If you had just arrived from Mars or Albuquerque, and walked past this charming, slightly bent over, white haired, cuddly grandfather type on the street, your first instinct would have been to embrace him as your long gone own grandpa.

Wrong.

His ever-present goons would have you taken out in a nanosecond. Didn't realize that they knew about nanoseconds, did you?

The Don's soft appearance belied his unyielding interior. Like Italian salami, he was delightful and garlicky on the outside but hard to the core. If you were foolish enough to anger him, a nanosecond would feel like an eternity in hell.

However, the Don was also a compassionate leader as long as you lovingly gave him anything he asked for, and never questioned it. In return he would grant special favors.

He was also still a confidant of, and beholden to the bidding of, King Victor Emanuel I. The years had only strengthened the familial bonds that had passed through so many generations. He never questioned or second-guessed any of the King's requests of him. In return, the Don had the absolute backing of Emanuel and, in turn, absolute control of his little fiefdom.

One particular example of their special relationship went back some 14 years to 1916, when on a clear September day Don Corezzo was summoned to King Victor Emanuel's palace in Rome, some 340 miles northeast. He was off the ferry and on the train to Rome within eight hours of receiving his King's request.

After swearing on his life that the story he was about to hear was not ever to be repeated to any third party without the King's explicit permission to do so, the following was revealed to him.

King Emanuel had but one son, the newborn Prince Giovanni. His subjects throughout the realm had rejoiced and celebrated with royal venison, wine and bread for the three days that had just ended the day before.

What was not known outside of a very restricted circle of confidants was that Emanuel's mistress, the beautiful Contessa Cornelia, had delivered yet another boy on the same day, almost at the same time as Prince Giovanni was delivered by the Queen.

This second child was simply named Pietro.

The King, being a very wise and compassionate man, did not want any future conflict as to a future heir to the throne, and so ordered that Pietro be quietly removed from the scene, but in a humane manner. There was a very special codicil appended to the Royal documents, attesting to this unique situation, and its resolution, that were to be sealed for three generations.

Don Corezzo was to be given the child and to select a good family to raise him in a kindly manner. They, too, were to be sworn to secrecy as to the true parentage of the child. Should any special monetary needs arise, Don Corezzo was ordered to respond to them in a compassionate manner.

Don Corezzo never wavered in any of his sworn responsibilities, just as his own "subjects" never disappointed him.

That sworn responsibility was to be the objective of Sandro's visit today.

CHAPTER 14

Sandro outlined his plan to the Don. He told him about his desire to further Pietro's education, something not only unavailable in Corezzo, but rarely even a dream in this farm area. It was also understood that if young Pietro was to rise beyond the ordinary, it could not happen in his Italy. There must never be any hint of a linkage to the throne. He asked if a small sum could be set aside to allow the boy to immigrate to that Golden Land, America.

Because of the close relationship of Don Corezzo and the King as well as the Don's innate intelligence and capability fortressed by acquaintances around the world, he was the ex-facto "Boss of Bosses," one hell of an important guy.

"Sandro, I understand Pietro's needs and the discreet manner in which it must be handled. I also appreciate your coming to me to help with the solution. It is my responsibility to see that the great King's orders, now my responsibility, are properly carried out with discretion and to the ultimate benefit of the boy.

Leave the matter in my hands, and come back to see me in three days' time."

After the many requisite thank-you gestures, Sandro and the miller walked back to the granary. There he picked up a well-rested and fed mule for the return journey to the farm.

Edward Gray

It was not often that Tommy Bonanno was honored with a direct transatlantic telephone call from Don Corezzo. That particular morning, he was extremely busy consolidating, read that as eliminating, some of his more contentious competition. The "Boss" of Staten Island was stepping on Tommy's toes in Manhattan, and that was not acceptable.

Bye-bye forever to the Staten Island "Boss," his Capo and Lieutenants.

But even that fun activity could not delay his answering this Call of Calls from the "Boss of Bosses."

"What a privilege and pleasure it is to receive this call from you. It brings me joy beyond description and unbound honor to my family."

"All right, Bonanno, cut the crap, here's what I want you to do, and all I am about to tell you is to be between you and me. Any other ears that hear about this will mean your quick and painful demise, along with your lovely wife and two boys. Capeesh?"

"Yes, Don Corezzo, all that you tell me goes no further."

"A young boy of 14 years will arrive in New York on the Liner "Andrea Doria" on October 18. His name is Pietro and he will be travelling alone. He is a simple farm boy and speaks no English. Use your influence to clear him through immigration control with a minimum of fuss. Your direct responsibility now becomes a bit more complicated. You are to have him placed with, and raised by, an upstanding "Non-Family" family. An interest bearing bank account with $100,000 is to be established in his name, to which he will have access after he completes college. Up to that point in time, you are to cover all of the costs associated with raising Pietro. Understand Bonanno?"

"Perfectly, Don Corezzo."

"He is to be taught English, educated and never to know this background. Are you still with me, Bonanno?"

"Si, my Don."

"Finally, he is not to be associated with you, your organization, or any other of a similar nature. He is not even to be made aware of who is behind this new life for him. Do I have your pledge that my orders will be followed without failure?"

"Of course, my Don. There is no room for failure to follow Don Corezzo's orders."

"Bonanno, I called you because I trust you to handle this delicate matter in an appropriate manner. On the day of the boy's graduation from college, in gratitude of your successful dedication to my request of you, you will find a significant contribution to your personal bank account. Additionally, there is a sealed letter to be opened at that time with specific instructions as to the boy's future wellbeing. Capeesh?"

"Si, and thank you for placing your faith in me. I will not fail you! As to the contribution to my account, that is not necessary, but I accept."

CHAPTER 15

Lieutenant Cornelius Collins was having the usual, another bad day.

It started when the alarm went off at his never wavering preset, 6:00 am wakeup time. Panic was always the immediate reaction to his having gone blind overnight. The feeling was partially dispelled when one eye finally managed to almost open. It further subsided when the other let some light in and became at least minimally functional.

The swamp in his mouth was a perfect complement to early morning dimmed vision as well as the absolute need to reach the bathroom before he created another swamp, in the bed.

Whew, he made it.

Connie should have learned some 22 years ago, when with a newly deepened voice and the need to shave first presented itself, that one must not approach such a delicate task with a sharp razor coupled with a fuzzy brain and eyesight. The results were very predictable and, as usual, did not disappoint on this morning. So, to limited vision and a crocodile infested mouth he now added a patchwork of bits and pieces of toilet paper to his face and neck. One day he would have to invest in a John Deere, or whatever it is called, electric shaver.

Connie was an aromatic and visual horror poster boy.

The worst part of this whole sordid approach to the new day was that this was the way it was almost every morning.

No wonder the brilliant Detective Lieutenant was still a bachelor. But I digress, as the really bad parts of his day were yet to come.

By 7:00 am, the shower, Crest toothpaste, nature's healing, and hot coffee did their respective jobs and he felt semi-alive.

The next step of this transformation to humanus erectus occurred during his morning routine eight-block brisk walk to the Midtown Precinct station house. Neither rain nor snow . . . etc. His first requisite stop was always at Coffee Ann's doughnut shop. His second cup of the morning waited for him on the counter along with the world's best chocolate-chocolate doughnut. Both were an absolute necessity to the re-entry ritual.

The next and final stop was at Gordie's Korner Kiosk, just two blocks from his Precinct, where folded copies of *The New York Times*, *The Daily News* and *The Post* awaited his arrival. The usual ritual morning greetings were exchanged.

Blind since birth, Gordie knew that the single bill passed to him by his long-term customer, Connie, was a fiver, and change was not expected.

By the time he entered the vintage '30's Precinct, Connie had become the picture of the professional Police Lieutenant that both his squad and superiors had come to know, respect and rely on.

They should only know that his revered thinking process was at this moment fixated on a chocolate-chocolate doughnut to the exclusion of everything else. But again, I digress.

The work day was about to begin, and Connie did not have the vaguest idea as to where to start it. The Met Murder, as it was known in the relentless public media, was now one week old and he was no closer to an answer then he was on day one.

Zilch.

Nada.

Thus, part two of Connie's bad day started.

CHAPTER 16

You know how people say that often dog owners resemble their dogs? I know a Chihuahua owner who . . . again I digress.

Well Connie had a desk that looked just like him immediately after he shaved. Bits of paper were strewn about with apparent abandon on every available surface, including the phone and the desk lamp. At least that was what it looked like to the casual observer. Actually, the sticky notes on his telephone were phone messages, the ones on his desktop computer were reminders as to where he had left off on his various Google, or Google-like quests, the one above his locked gun drawer was a reminder to spray deodorant on his bulletproof vest, and the rest covered the range from shopping lists to schedules and deadlines.

Connie should have had a bulldog, as he mimicked that animal's perseverance and strength. The task at hand was the task at hand! The jaws of his mind would not let go of the problem "du jour" regardless of what went on around him: the time of day (or night), mealtimes, conversations, or his too-few dates with the opposite sex. Yes, he was heterosexual, when he had time for distractions from his current professional quest.

There was that one time when he was preparing for the blind date that Watkins had set him up with.

As usual, shaving didn't go all that well and the second drawer failed to come up with clean shirt. No time to pick up the load of everything he owned waiting for him at Lee's Laundry around the corner so, with the application of the old remedy using a Tide stain remover stick, a hot iron and a spray of deodorant, he was quasi-presentable.

Lucy (short for Lucia) was quite lovely. Most importantly, Lucy was of the same stock as Connie. Both had Italian grandparents and were almost Catholic, but to the core.

Short black hair framed her oval face that needed almost zero war paint to enhance her natural beauty. Piercing dark brown eyes radiated her intelligence and inquisitiveness while completely absorbing and processing you, and you alone.

It was not exactly a negative that she had a body that was as far from masculine as one can get. I believe I mentioned that Connie was definitely heterosexual.

None of that magnificent example of that perfect female in front of him was overlooked by his inner being.

Dinner was delightful. He even almost remembered what he ate. It was difficult to slice his steak without ever once taking his eyes off Lucy until she excused herself to go to the necessary.

The inside of his head rumbled with questions without answers about the rest of the evening:

Should I or shouldn't I ask her back to my place?

Did I leave it in a mess?

Will she, or won't she?

How about her place?

Is it too soon?

Etc., etc.

It was during the course of his fantasizing that the random thoughts from somewhere else in the ether entered his one-track brain.

Conditions for a serious brain overload collision.

Why was Enrico murdered in one place and then transported to the Met to be discovered?

What was the significance of the Met?

Why were these questions coming up now?

Why were they imposing on his more immediate and much more important fantasy about Lucy? Which should I screw this evening, my work, or Lucy?

The answer was obvious, screw both.

And so, he did.

At about four in the morning, with this unbelievable sleeping body pressed up against him, Connie decided that Lucy was definitely a keeper—but so were his earlier thoughts about the Met.

It was time to return from the delights of the sublime to the mundane depths of the real world that consumed the rest of his waking hours.

Connie slipped out of bed without disturbing Lucy's deep sleep. He wanted to go home, shower, shave, etc., when he realized that he was at home.

It was too early to wake Lucy, but his endorphins were now all fired up and the varied questions about the Met bouncing around the inside of his cranium would not allow him to return to the bed.

That damned single track was at work again.

As quietly as possible Connie closed the bathroom door, showered his epidermis, drained the nightly accumulation of swamp from his mouth masking it with Crest and finally nicked new sites on his face for the tissue-pasting ritual. He could not leave the bathroom for another ten minutes. He had to wait for the nicks to stop bleeding so that he could remove the paper patches. No sense frightening the poor girl that early in the morning and ruining their relationship.

On the way to the kitchen, Connie took note of the rising/falling belly on the body in the bed. In his profession one automatically checked for signs of life! She was definitely alive, but still recovering in slumberville.

Some twenty minutes later, a vision entered the kitchen, gave him a kiss on the cheek and a long good-morning embrace. Connie returned to planet Earth and escorted her to the table he had just finished setting for breakfast.

The table was laden with:

orange juice to complement her freshness,
sunny-side up eggs to reflect her disposition,
bacon to echo her well-done exterior, and
coffee so that the apartment smelled right.

He hoped she would not notice his dishes, none of which matched each other. They were a perfect complement to the silver, which shared a non-similar, non-relationship. However, Connie was not entirely without taste. The two Brawny paper towels used as napkins did match each other, as did the two Dunkin Donuts coffee mugs.

As one would surmise, none of this was lost on Lucy. However there was no contest. Who would opt for a matched set of china over the perfect lover?

Besides, the breakfast was delicious.

Connie then did something he had never before done. As a token of their nascent relationship he presented a pair of perfectly matched pearl earrings dangling from gold clips that had once belonged to his mother, to Lucy. Tears of joy were her thank-you as they once again embraced.

Plans were made to meet for dinner at seven that evening, but with each giving the same caveat, "I could be late or may even have to cancel at the last minute."

As a lawyer for Chen, O'Brien, Hernandez, Elgin and Nozzerotti (C.O.H.E.N. Ltd.), Lucy often had to work around the clock to meet the demands of the court and/or her client. Her firm, of which she and 26 others were limited partners, had an intriguing background. It was formed 19 years ago by the two Cohen brothers. Lee was a Harvard Law School graduate and Ben graduated with the same degree from Yale Law School two years later. There was always the argument between the two competitive institutions as to which was the better "Same degree."

They formed the firm as a partnership, each holding 50% of the equity. The other nameplate "lawyers" never existed. They correctly felt that the varied ethnic backgrounds implied by the names would draw varied clients.

Boy did that ever work!

In the following years, as their client base grew, they added limited partners and backup lawyers to handle the ever-growing caseload. That is how Lucy was hired and eventually promoted to a limited partnership. She earned every penny of the million or so that she had accumulated during her seven sixteen-hour days per week over the years. The Cohen brothers were not exactly financially hurting either.

Needless to say, Connie had the same time restraints as Lucy, except that his clients never spoke directly to him. His interpreter was almost always the forensic Medical Examiner, so that was Connie's next move.

After an extended "Fare-Thee-Well" with Lucy, Connie had Watkins drive him to the corner of Second Avenue and 28th Street, where New York's newly suspiciously deceased arrived around the clock, but mostly in the very early am hours. In his office at the City Medical Examiner's Office, Dr. Hochschuler, set aside 37 minutes of his very limited time to brief Connie on his findings. It was one of those very rare occasions that demanded Hochschuler's direct involvement, but this was a very high profile case and the media would not let go of it.

The U.S. was in between Middle-East invasions, hurricanes, elections, sex scandals and gang wars, so Connie's murder had become the time and space filler needed to sell toothpaste, prescription drugs, cars and insurance to the public. It hit the national and international news as a relief from the other catastrophic happenings. The unusual conditions of the murder caught the public's attention. Unknown to the authorities, it also caught the eyes of those paying for this extermination.

The direct pressure on Connie for immediate resolution was more than he had ever experienced, and weighed heavily on him. It not only interfered with his Lucy daydreams but, as we all expected, was to delay tonight's rendezvous with her . . . for several days.

CHAPTER 17

"To reinforce my early conclusions, if you look at the coloration of his skin, it definitely suggests suffocation. The noose was caught on his chin and did not break or constrict the trachea. It certainly would not have been a contributor to his death.

Ergo, he was dead before he was hanged.

To refresh your memory, there was the slight odor that one could just about make out in his mouth that we had identified as sodium pentafolinate. I believe that it was applied directly to his face causing immediate unconsciousness. It was probably administered in complete surprise, as there are no bruises suggesting a struggle. The killer was no stranger. He knew the victim, or had an introduction to him. The poor guy had no idea he was about to die.

It also falls in line with the concierge's report that the killer was expected.

His visit also confirms my estimated time of death.

We further determined that a few strands of red hair found on a pillow were synthetic and were probably from a hairpiece or the false beard worn by the killer. He either wore gloves or was very careful about wiping all surfaces that he touched.

There were so many shoe prints in the carpet because of the recent parade of movers and decorators that it was impossible to isolate any that could be useful. In other words, we have nothing useful for you other than you are dealing with a very professional, probably contract killer.

Sorry that I haven't anything more for you to work on, Connie."

"Thanks, Doc."

Chapter 18

The squad room was about 1,620 feet square, walls painted a sort of mottled teal, whatever color that is. There were ten battered steel desks in two rows in the center, a holding cage on the right, bathrooms for use by those outside of the cage, through a door on the left wall. A stainless-steel toilet was located inside the cage. Windows on the right wall overlooked a narrow alley. A huge corkboard plus a giant electronic screen was located on the south side. The screen was capable of projecting TV and/or computer images. The south side door led to the second-floor hallway.

This was command central for Connie's homicide group activity.

It was almost constantly inundated by 102+ decibel "conversations" across the room, the incessant ringing of phones, computers beeping, chairs scraping on the rough wood floor, metal desk drawers clanging shut, a whopper of a fart, the occasional "Oh shit, I got a paper cut on my finger," the bad cough and its mandatory follow-up sneezes, steel garbage can lids banging in the alley below, the rattling last gasps of the ancient room air-conditioner, rap music leaking from someone's earphones, all harmoniously joined by the ever-present wheedling and ranting from the cage.

Not exactly a place for quiet contemplation.

However, contemplation, quiet or not, was what was now needed and was the reason that all ten members of Connie's squad were assembled.

There was a high-profile murder to be solved, and after three days, a starting point was still needed.

"All right, settle down and let's get moving. Here is what we know," and he proceeded to summarize all of the facts, as they knew them. When he mentioned the red wig business there was a gasp in the holding pen.

The noise came out of the small pinched face of Louie Bartelomo, a petty drug dealer they had picked up the night before. This was not the first time he had been in this particular cage, which he affectionately called his second home. As he had more than once been indicted, this home was more important, bigger and cleaner than the sty he lived in the rest of the time. The food was also better. So much for the lifestyles of the not so rich and infamous!

Watkins picked up on this and interrupted Connie mid-sentence. "What's bugging you, Louie? We're old friends, come clean."

"*Nuttin*, Watkins."

"Come on, out with it or you will find yourself in the big cage downstairs. You know the one I mean, the stockyard filled with all of your favorite animals—the ones that you owe *mucho lira* to. Then all of our minders will go out for a nice long coffee break while you meet new old friends. Capeesh?"

"Yeah, yeah, I get the *pitcher*. I'll fill you in *wid wad* I know if you just keep me in this *loverly* B&B for *anudder day* or two."

"I'll use my influence, but only if you're not just jerking me around and have some real info. Move the lips."

"OK, OK! You know my office on Second Avenue and 25th Street, *Moiphy's* beverage emporium?"

"Right," said Watkins, "*Murphy's Bar and Grill*. A bar it is, but the only grilling I have ever seen there was me grilling you and some of your buddies. Not exactly the image one has of a corporate office. Go on."

Louie went on, "We got our *regerlers*, Mario, Bruno, Vittorio, De Lucca, and the rest of *Moiphy's* Irish business associates. I know. You asked me once before about the Irish part. They are all as Irish as Francesco *Moiphy*."

"Get to the point, Louie."

"OK, OK! About *tree* weeks ago, I *seen* this dude that I ain't ever seen before. He walks in and asks for Vittorio. He obviously never met him before because he was standing right in front of him! I points to Vittorio and the two of them huddle at the corner table for about a half hour."

"I get the picture," says Watkins, "but what do these two lovers have to do with the price of beans in Tibet?"

"*Gotcher, dats a gud* one," Louie says, "but I was *gettin* to my point. The *udder* guy had a really bad hairpiece, and it was a real scary red! It looked like it was dipped in blood or in paint left over by Mark Rothko, or some *udder* painter guy. I knows color since I spend so much time at MOMA *watchen* all *dem* paintings. I *specially* admire *dis* Rothko *boid*, a great field colorist *wid* great space proportions and symbiotic harmonies intensely juxtaposed on his canvases. Sort of gestalt, gestural brush movements."

"Hm," mused Watkins, "What is it they say about a book and its cover? Louie has a lot of hidden pages."

"Were you able to overhear any of their conversation?"

"*Nah, dey wuz* too far away, and I *wuzent intrested.*"

"Louie, if you can pick this guy out of mug shots and discretely point out Vittorio, I believe we can have a deal. Want to give it a shot?"

"*Shur*, why not, but do I still get my bologna sandwich for lunch today?"

CHAPTER 19

After some 4 ½ hours of looking at *pitchers*, er pictures, no ID.

Watkins called in the sketch artist to get a rendering of Redhead's face. "*Da nose was a little bigger. Not wider, longer. Not as long as Cyrano de what's-his-name. De eyes wuz bluer, like Monet's "Water Lilies" pond, widout de algae. Gud, I tink youz got it. By God youz got it.*"

The drawing was then scanned into the Facial Recognition computer.

After several hours running time, it was not recognized in their database.

Connie then signed the necessary authorization papers to have the search expanded to the FBI, CIA and Interpol computer bases. This was not as complex an undertaking as one might assume. The drawing is electronically sent to each of the other's servers by using the proper codes, automatically starting the new searches.

It was less than ten minutes when a "Hit" was electronically sent from Interpol back to Connie's computer. At the same time, notification of the "Hit" was sent to all interested law enforcement parties around the world. This was pretty much to everybody because the ID was that of a most-wanted international hit man, known as Charlie Mallard or whatever his real name might be. There was also a list of other aliases he had been known to use.

A long list.

Apparently, Charlie was a professional assassin wanted in multiple countries for unsolved murders of high profile people. Just as in this case, they knew the murderer but not the "why" or who hired him. He was on the Top Ten Interpol list, and no closer to capture than he was some ten or twelve years ago, when he first came to international attention.

This was one bad dude that Connie and his team were up against.

With his background, it was apparent that this murder was not a simple grudge, but involved some really serious motive and even more serious money! Not some simple lovers spat. Enrico's demise was extremely important to someone or someones.

His facial recognition was based on a picture taken by a surveillance camera in Montecatine Square, immediately after the horrific assassination of Deputy Minister Ciglioni on May 16, 2009.

It was one of those beautiful spring days in Rome, the sun shining brightly, with crowds there to enjoy the day and to greet the very popular Minister. Sounds of laughter and approval were roared by the massive group of admirers. Ciglioni was smiling and radiated happiness with every step while frequently stopping to shake hands with his admirers. He was followed by his lovely wife of 26 years and their three movie star grade children, when a red spot suddenly appeared on his forehead.

He slumped to the ground, dead.

As quick as that!

Although the police and bystanders knew which direction the shot came from, no one had actually heard it or seen the gunman. The rifle, a 547 Colt, produced primarily for US Army sniper teams, was found some thirty meters away stuffed into a litter basket, along with a man's jacket. No fingerprints, manufacturing number, or other identifiable remnants were found. It had been externally modified to resemble a cane! The jacket was equally "clean."

The police team scanned all of the surveillance tapes in and around the square, concentrating on the area near the litter basket. About a half hour prior to the shooting an elderly gray haired/bearded man, using a cane, was noted strolling among the trees adjacent to the litter basket. Immediately after the shooting, a young redheaded jogger ran by. The features on both faces were identical.

In retrospect, it was obviously the same person.

He had never been caught.

Not even a sighting.

CHAPTER 20

Connie, presiding, said, "Watkins, now that we know what Charlie looks like, liaise with the Federal and Municipal Transportation authorities. Coordinate facial recognition scanning of all passengers in all airports, tri-state terminals and stations as well as in other public places. Also, arrange for posters and handouts with his face on it to be distributed. Move."

Ozzie received a copy of all of the files that Interpol and the CIA had on Charlie.

He spent the next 24 hours reading and re-reading every single scrap of paper and electronic file. He checked to see if he could isolate patterns, such as aliases, methodology, spending habits, lodging preferences, eating habits, women (or men) associated with him, employers, etc. Also, to see if there was any background as to his ethnicity, parentage and education. Anything that popped out of the pages.

He also gave a copy to Doc Hochschuler for psychological analysis. Steve might be able to shed some light on Charlie's basic needs. Such needs usually require some sort of satisfaction, which in turn could help predict where he might show up. He could be into sushi or hookers or chess or fast cars or old movies or other distinctive traits. It could open other paths to follow.

"The rest of you, continue with your investigations and report back to me at eight tonight."

CHAPTER 21

He was still alive and active in his chosen profession because of his rigid training, experience and instincts. A rare combination that had allowed him to exist on this side of the grass after some 20 years pursuing an occupation that has a life expectancy usually measured in hours or days, certainly not in years or decades.

He had no old friends. Come to think of it, other than the probable occasional one-night stand, he didn't even have new friends. Family was essentially non-existent. His parents died of natural causes within seven months of each other some eleven years ago. Of course, he was on assignment each time and could not attend their funerals. Even if he were free it would have been impossible for him to be there. The close family attendees thought he had died in the war years ago, others were not even aware that he had ever existed. It was also likely that one or more of the "mourners" were there hoping to ID him so that they could quickly dispatch him to join his parents.

After a less than brilliant four years in high school, Anthony (his apparent real name, and not one of the many acquired names, such as Charlie) had but one course open to him: The US Army.

After all, he resented working in conventional workplaces and did not play well with others. He tended to bully those who did not bully him. For one year as a grunt he took all of the abuse hurled at him. As he matured, he began to show a certain brilliance on the firing range and in hand-to-hand combat training.

Bullying abruptly stopped.

His lethal skills were soon noted and he was offered a position in a newly formed secret Department of Defense Assault and Rescue Team, code named DART. This group would some years in the future evolve into the elite Green Berets.

One hundred and twenty handpicked recruits to this new unit were secreted to a camp well hidden within 120,000 acres of nothing but acres of acres within the Smoky Mountains in Georgia. The closely-knit team spent their time totally out of touch with anyone beyond the camp enclosure, perfecting silent assault skills using various armaments, sniping, manual close combat and other kill basics. Anthony was a natural and was soon promoted to unit leader.

He taught his men how to silently kill without a weapon other than one's own hands. If necessary, how to create a weapon out of tools, cutlery, dishes, linens, plastic bottles, toothbrushes, soap, condoms and most anything else found in an average home.

After a year, the team, led by Anthony, received its first assignment directly from the White House. It involved an "invisible" incursion into a certain Middle-East country (still classified), to the house of a certain General Al Harabi (a pseudonym), the commandant of their secret service. They were to take him out (not out of the country, but as in out of life).

It was a complete success.

You never read about it, just as you never read about their subsequent missions over the years, because "they didn't happen."

After five years, Anthony was recruited by the CIA to join their black ops team. Arrangements were made for his honorable discharge from the military and transfer to the "Farm" near Williamsburg, Virginia. There he was steeped in CIA methodology and additional lethal skills.

Anthony spent the next ten years with the agency as a specialist assassin. He almost always worked alone, and accomplished every mission with a minimum of fuss and mess.

After the aforementioned ten years, he began to realize that although he was adept at and enjoyed his work, he really was not providing for his own future. He needed to start some sort of nest egg for old age, if he made it that far.

So, Anthony left officially sanctioned government work for the more lucrative private industry.

What was then left in life for this poor soul without a protective sponsor? Only the three things he valued most:

An occupation he truly enjoyed.

Solitude.

Lots and lots and lots of money.

Anthony, his true name, the one given to him by his late parents, was never used again after he left the "Agency" and also after some Interpol close calls. He had piles of passports, driver's licenses, birth certificates, credit cards, mobile phones, other ID, all under different names and physical characteristics. There were now also multi-millions of cash in various currencies divided, under different identities and passwords, in at least a dozen bank vaults around the world.

He had no monetary need driving him to accept yet another assignment, other than the excitement of it. That was what he craved—no, he needed. There were no loving spouse or children, no birthday presents to give or receive, no Thanksgiving or Christmas dinners, no drinking buddy and certainly no confidant.

That was what the common masses craved.

Not Anthony.

He had his assassinations, occasional assignations and other fun things.

Could there be anything more fulfilling than the requisite meticulous planning with no one to bounce ideas off other than your own intellect?

Was anything more thrilling than the execution of the execution?

Any other questions?

CHAPTER 22

It was well into the third week since Enrico's senseless murder that Elaine felt the urgent need to re-establish some sort of routine so that every waking moment wasn't spent on replaying those horrid, but still so very fresh memories. The jolting notification, the morbid identification, the all-encompassing suspicions, the endless questions by others, and especially those bouncing around in Mobius circles within her own mind. There was absolutely nothing further she could contribute to the ongoing investigation. She had recalled, recollected, sensed and then searched deeper and deeper, but could not expand on what was already known to the investigators. If she didn't begin to live again, she was afraid she would soon join Enrico in death.

With these forces driving her, Elaine once again began her memorization of the Lady's Maid role in the libretto for *La Traviata*. Her introduction to the Metropolitan Opera stage was set for December 11, in six months. If she didn't start now, her lifelong singing career momentum could be lost. She had even set a voice lesson appointment with Mme. Kordovanska for the next Thursday. All of this resurrected activity was to become her sanity preserver.

Her life had to get back on track.

There goes the phone yet again, she said to herself. *Why can't the press leave me alone? However, it could be Lt. Connie, with more information.*

"Hello?"

"Ms Marker, this is Charles Welling, Managing Partner of Smithson, Welling, Schwartz, Thompson and Caroccio, Ltd. I wonder if I could have a word with you about a very important and extremely confidential matter of direct concern to you?"

"Your firm is a well-known and respected group. What is this all about, Mr. Welling?"

"I'm afraid that this is a matter that is so delicate in nature, it cannot be addressed over the phone, or in any insecure place, as it has to do with recent events in your life. It would be best if you could join me in my office, perhaps this afternoon at three, if convenient to you.

For your own wellbeing, please do not tell any one of your impending visit other than Lt. Collins. He must be made aware of all of your plans until the investigation into your late fiancé's death has been resolved. As a matter of fact, he is planning to join us.

Additionally, when you arrive, please identify yourself as "Ms Jones." That is the only name that will be known to my staff."

"I don't know what this is all about, but it sounds compelling so I will plan to be there at 3:00." She immediately called Connie and told him about the call. He asked if she wanted a police escort, which she declined. However, he did confirm that he planned to see her at 3:00 that afternoon.

As with most midtown locations, the Smithson, et al office was but a five-minute cab ride from her own building.

385 Madison Avenue was an imposing 20-story, gray stone, older office building that had once housed several of the larger advertising agencies. That was in the 1950's and '60's, when the name Madison Avenue was synonymous with the advertising industry. The Mad Men subsequently moved to the Flatiron District, named for the famous late 19th century corner building shaped like the familiar triangular flat iron.

385 Madison Avenue soon became home to the 562 partners, plus some 1,200 support staff, of Smithson, et al, one of the big five New York City law groups.

This outfit was obviously not the corner-store ambulance chaser group.

She whirled through one of the revolving doors and approached the huge marble desk with a very attractive young blond receptionist behind it. At least the ode to art deco and beauty had not changed from the old Mad Men days.

"My name is Jones and I have an appointment with Mr. Welling."

"Yes, Ms Jones, Mr. Welling and another gentleman are awaiting your visit and are in his third-floor office. Liz will escort you there."

Charles Welling's third floor corner office was very "Old World Executive Brown," with plush overstuffed brown leather chairs, a brown leather couch and walls papered in, guess what, matching browns and puce (still have no idea what puce looks like.) A brownish tinted world globe, about two feet in diameter, sat next to one of the chairs. A brown leather-topped desk that could have served as a landing strip for 747's with room for hangers, was situated next to the windows. The coffee table (shades of brown tile, of course) was strewn with the latest copies of *Yachting Today* and *National Parks*.

Interestingly enough, she recognized the central painting on the long wall as being by the same artist, Barbara Gray, as the art that Rico had loved. It was brownish, and appeared to be some sort of collage of used coffee filters.

Coincidence?

Why in his collection too?

Welling opened with, "Welcome, Ms Jones, and again, that is the only name that you will be known by in this office. You of course know Lt. Collins. He and I are at this time the only ones aware of your true identity, and we plan to keep it that way. No one, including my secretary and partners, will ever know you as anyone else! That also includes the police department, other than Lt. Collins. His assistant and confidant, Sergeant Francis DiAngelo will also soon be made aware of this arrangement. As you become more informed as to the purpose of this visit, I believe you will agree to this strange request.

Please make yourself comfortable on the couch. Would you like coffee, tea or any other drink?"

"No, thank you, l am just so extremely anxious to hear what you have to say. This is all so mysterious. As you might expect I have had enough intrigue in the past few weeks."

"Ms Jones, what I am about to tell you is about your deceased fiancé, and I hasten to say does not reflect negatively at all on him. It is a story about his heritage and how it affected him and how it could potentially affect you. This story absolutely must not leave this room. It cannot be related to others, including the police, under any circumstances, unless previously cleared with me. As I noted, the only exceptions are Lt. Collins and his deputy, Detective Sergeant DiAngelo, who will be privy to all we discuss. He has also agreed not to release any information given to him confidentially, unless released to do so by me.

I must have your verbal agreement before I can continue."

A now very pale Elaine agreed.

Wellington continued, "This narrative goes back some 80 years to the small town of Cortezzo de Marino, Italy," and he proceeded to tell her about Enrico's grandfather's encounter with the Godfather, the delivery of the baby boy, and the subsequently arranged relationship on behalf of King Emanuel 1.

The narrative continued, with certain un-named go-betweens to Enrico's deceased father, without any significant changes through the years. Most particularly, he spoke about the effect it had on Enrico. He was recently made well aware of his background and was prepared to tell you all about it prior to setting a wedding date.

The three of us are three of but six people in the United States who are now aware of this story. The fourth will be Sergeant DiAngelo, when he is read into the details. The fifth person, who shall remain nameless, pays my retainer.

The sixth person I believe to be Enrico's murderer."

She interrupted the story, "I don't understand why Enrico was murdered some 80 years after the events you just related, and why are you telling me this now?"

Welling went on. "Your late fiancé visited me just two months ago and made out his will leaving his considerable fortune to you. As significant as it is, it is miniscule in comparison to what is still at stake.

Are you sure you don't need a drink of water?"

"No, please go on."

Welling continued, "One of the codicils of King Emanuel's will was to hold his personal fortune intact and to divide it among his living direct heirs exactly 80 years, to the day, after his death. That date arrives on June 30 this year."

Elaine interjected, "Enrico is dead, and I can assure you that I am most certainly not a direct descendent."

Welling went on, "My firm has an excellent investigative branch that reports only to the partner with a need to know and had requested said investigation. In this case, that is me. Their findings go no further than me. The investigator is legally bound to respect this restriction. If there is need for him to testify during a trial, or relay information to outside authorities, only the partner involved may release him to do so.

If you agree to accept my assistance, which has all been paid for by the unnamed person who has retained my services, I will continue with the narrative, which definitely does still affect you."

A confused Elaine said, "I do agree to the use of your professional services. Please continue."

She signed the appropriate documents appointing Charles Welling of Smithson, et al as her attorney. Lt Collins was the witness.

Welling then went on, "My private investigator, has informed me that via information he has covertly secured, you are pregnant, and are likely carrying Enrico's child. Your child, subject to DNA testing, will prove to be a direct descendant of King Emanuel 1 of Italy, and as such could be the recipient of an estimated $2.5 billion-dollar portfolio."

After what seemed like a six-hour pause, actually only about 20 seconds, an extremely pale Elaine weakly murmured, "Yes, I am pregnant, and I have no idea how this information became known to your investigator other than by my gynecologist or my manager."

Oh my god, she immediately realized, *it was my manager, Cyril Stenta, the Yenta.*

"You did say billion, as in billion?"

"Yes, Ms Jones. The number is approximate as we have not yet had the opportunity to audit the portfolio, but will do so in due course. However, we have reason to believe that it should be in that ballpark."

Ballpark? That is a nation!

Welling continued, "The actual amount in the portfolio is about twice what I had mentioned, but there is one other direct heir in the picture, Prince Emanuel II, directly descended from Queen Regina, Emanuel I's wife. Here is where the picture becomes very cloudy. We have learned that the current Prince Emanuel was made aware of Enrico's existence about a year ago and his potential claim to part of the fortune. It seems that the current Emanuel does not have the reputation of being the sharing type.

It is reported that his wish is to have the entire $5 billion, not a meager $2.5 billion. I'm not sure that I would be able to see the difference, but that's only me.

It is the opinion of my retainer-paying client and me that this could be the motive behind the murder of Enrico. Lt. Collins has been made aware of this and is obviously following up. People have killed for a lot less."

Welling went on, "It is with the above in mind that I have prepared a list of actions, subject to your approval and acceptance, to be taken to safeguard you and your heir-to-be, as well as assisting Lt. Collins in his investigation."

Elaine sat back in her chair and said, "My head is like a spinning mass of cotton candy trying to assimilate all you have said, before it melts. Please, a glass of water is now really needed."

After a few sips followed by moments of information ingestion, Elaine went on, "May I see your list?"

Welling went to his wall safe, hidden behind Barbara Gray's collage, dialed in eight numbers, opened it and removed a sheaf of papers in a plain white folder simply marked "Jones." He opened it, removed the top pieces, and passed them to Elaine.

He then said, "Please take your time to look it over and then let's discuss each item. It is essential that the protocol stated, with only very minor adjustments, be adhered to. Without such agreement, the life of your as-yet-unborn child and, of course, yourself, would be at great risk. I might add that Lt. Collins is in complete agreement."

Elaine took the papers and tried to digest the impact of the eight items that screamed out at her. After some ten minutes, she looked at Welling and said, "What you are suggesting is not a life, but a life sentence! How could I possibly accept the conditions you specify?"

Welling then stood up, his full 6'3" frame towering over the still seated, petite Elaine. The well-practiced attorney's stance was softened by the shock of silver white hair conveying a lifetime of accumulated intelligence, coupled with a soft resonant voice that communicated compassion, friendliness and protection. It was quite clear how Welling became senior partner of one of the world's most prestigious law firms.

He looked down at Elaine and said, "Before you jump to any conclusions, let us first discuss each item. Why it is there, how it would work and what the impact would be on you. I believe that then, and only then, will you be able to see how it could truly affect your future wellbeing. Remember, more than your life could depend on it.

May we continue?"

Elaine responded, "I am certainly prepared to listen."

She once again picked up the piece of paper that would transform her.

Item 1 *Elaine must vanish!*

Welling elaborated, "The intent is quite simple. Elaine must completely vanish. No one, other than Lt. Collins, Sergeant DiAngelo and me will know who you are, where you are and how to contact you.

If you so agree, tomorrow morning you will use the kit in the plain blue cloth bag left in your apartment bathroom by my agent, to change your appearance. Place the wig over your own hair, insert the color changing contact lenses, wear the non-prescription dark framed glasses and don the very high heeled shoes and brightly colored dress we left on your bed. You are now Ms Norah Jones! Your real hair change will have to wait until you have the time in a day or for us to arrange a discreet and very professional beauty counselor appointment.

Practice speaking in a lower voice timbre. I'm sure that your years of voice training will assist you in this task.

Take absolutely nothing from your apartment with you. If it does not fit in the small purse we left for you, leave it behind. Anything you must have from the apartment will be brought to your new location by the end of the day.

When you leave your current residence do not greet anyone by name, just smile and sign thank you to the concierge and the doorman. They will smile back, but not recognize you.

When you reach the curb, a dark blue Mercedes Benz sedan will be waiting and Alex, your chauffeur, will greet you as Ms Jones and then drive you to your new apartment in the upper east eighties. He will drive directly into the garage, escort you through the lobby, introduce you to the concierge as the new tenant, Ms Jones, and then escort you directly to your new apartment.

Alex, or one of his assistants, will be at your service 24/7. Beyond being your chauffeur, he is one of our top security officers, with a hand-picked team that will offer round-the-clock protection. He will appraise Lt. Collins and/or Sergeant DiAngelo, of any anomalies.

All of your living expenses will be covered by our firm during this period. We will also dispose of your current apartment and any contents not essential to you.

Let's leave questions until we have gone through all eight items, as they are all interrelated."

A very confused Elaine almost whispered, "I'm not sure why I have to vanish, but I agree to hold back discussing the items until the end."

Item 2 *Ms Jones must place her career ambitions on a "Back Burner" until all is resolved.*

Welling elaborated, "It is not very difficult to feel your reaction to item 2, and I can sense your combination of inner void, indignation and fear of losing your life's dream. Before we discuss it further at the end of the list, let me reassure you that this will only be an interruption for a finite period of time, not a closure."

Item 3 *Ms Jones will not be in direct contact with any relatives or friends. Any spontaneous contact by these individuals will not be acknowledged by Ms Jones.*

With tears in her eyes, Elaine pleaded, "I have already lost the one I love most! You now propose taking the "me" from me, and then removing all of the others I love, cherish and need. This goes beyond what might have had a glimmer of reasonableness. It is insane. I need the support of those I love and trust."

Welling once again responded with, "I understand your frustration and ask you to bear with me until the end. At that point we will be able to discuss and modify conditions to ease the burden, but not put your life in danger."

Item 4 *Ms Jones will change all of her health professionals.*

Welling immediately told her that all of her records would be securely transmitted to the new caregivers under her new name. He also said that he would recommend top people in the fields of her needs.

Item 5 *All of Ms Jones's credit cards, licenses, and insurance coverages will be cancelled and replaced.*

He said that new photo credit cards, ID's, licenses and insurance coverage, all under her new name and image would be handled by his company and issued to her, within days. Similarly, new bank accounts and lines of credit would be provided.

Item 6 *Electronic devices and transmissions will be regulated and secured.*

Welling expanded, "This means that we will replace your cell phone, computer and any other electronic devices you may require with new units that have been made secure from hackers and will be monitored to insure there are no intruders. Needless to say, no Facebook, Twitter or any other electronic social interaction.

Item 7 *Ms Jones will not venture beyond her apartment front door without a security escort.*

Welling noted, "Said escort will be one provided by me or my agent. On occasion, you may be asked by Lt. Collins to attend certain meetings, at which time he will bear the responsibility to provide such protection and the secret of your true identity. In Lt. Collins' absence, his deputy, Sergeant DiAngelo will be totally available to you."

Connie nodded in agreement.

Item 8 *You will not respond to any telephone, electronic communication or casual conversation other than as Ms Norah Jones.*

"There is no need for further clarification on this item, is there?"
The nod of her head was enough of a response.
Welling went on, "I fully understand your reaction to all of the above, but now let's see if we can put your mind at least partially at ease under these grueling and extreme precautions.

Our objectives are threefold.

The first and foremost is to insure the safety of you and the child you are carrying.

The second is to set the scenario for the identification and capture of your fiancé's killer.

The third is the capture of the killer's employer, and the course of justice for all involved.

I will not step back from my responsibility and commitments until all three goals have been met."

After another drink of water and some time for Elaine, soon to be Norah, to try to collect and organize the exploding thoughts saturating her head, the discussion continued.

"Before we go any further, to help put your mind partially at ease, I repeat for you to please understand that the "Vanishing Act" will only be for a very finite period of time. Elaine will re-emerge as soon as the murderer is identified, his intent toward you thwarted, his employer captured and both are in police custody. Obviously, I cannot give you a time scale."

Elaine nodded and said, "I do understand that the timing of the above cannot be predicted, but I am not sure how long I can live under those conditions. I also understand that Elaine disappearing could be my life preserver however, convenience versus death is a no-brainer.

Shall we continue?"

Welling went on, "Item 1 is an absolute must. You must not be recognized by your most intimate friends. Your whole persona must change. For example, the sweet melodious-voiced, petite Elaine known to all who have crossed her path will now be taller, gruff and overbearing. No more Ms "Nice Guy." It is contrary to everything you have grown to be, but that's the whole idea—at least until this whole matter is completely resolved."

The actress in Elaine accepted Item 1 with a dismissive nod of the head coupled with a haughty, low-pitched grunt. In a lower register voice she said, "Let's move on to Item 2. Does that mean no voice lessons at all?"

Welling picked up, "You can sing in the shower to your heart's content. You can continue to memorize librettos, movements, stage directions, etc. However, no formal lessons until this is resolved. To answer your unasked question, it is unadvisable to go to another voice coach during this period.

She may recognize your voice quality and ask too many questions. Much too risky.

Again, always try to keep in mind that this is for a finite period of time."

He continued, "I recognize that Item 3 is a real bitch, but a really important bitch."

Elaine almost shouted, "I can't just talk to myself. There must be other people in my life or I will go stark raving mad. Someone must be at the other end of my telephone calls, dinners have to be shared, conversations are more than just between me and my inner being, and excursions are usually shared with another human being.

Who will be there outside of my abandoned head?"

Welling replied, "Lt. Collins and Sgt. DiAngelo and myself will always be available as sounding boards to vent your ideas and frustrations."

Ms Jones, already accepting her new role, continued, "Another problem is what will be told to those I know and love? What about my parents and brothers, for example? My voice coach! The Metropolitan Opera! They will be more than a little concerned that I have suddenly dropped off the face of this planet. I believe that if I should suddenly disappear, they will start police probes and a publicity campaign to locate me. How will that be handled?"

Welling reached into the folio that he had previously removed from the wall safe and handed Elaine several other pieces of paper for her perusal. "These are suggestions as to what you might want to handwrite and mail to each person of concern. It explains that because of your recent loss and the persistent hounding by the press, you have decided to take an extended solo vacation abroad for an indefinite period of time. You will write them at irregular intervals, but do not want the obligation of continued communication. You must have a lot of rest and alone time. The general wording has been approved by Lt. Collins.

As you will see, the wording of the letters to the Metropolitan Opera and to your voice coach state a similar reasoning but go on to say that upon your return you would appreciate if they could once again give you the opportunity to resume your nascent career where you had left off.

Again, these are just outlines to be rewritten in your own style and handwriting. We will assume the obligation of posting these initial letters and in the future will mail them from various parts of the world.

Questions?"

Elaine scanned the drafts without specific comment and indicated that she would read them in detail that evening, redraft, handwrite and give them to Alex in the morning for a final wording security check by Welling before posting the initial ones.

Welling and Collins nodded in agreement.

Welling wished Ms Jones well and told her, "I will keep you apprised of investigation progress as it occurs. However, as I may not be available 24 hours a day, Lt. Collins or Sgt. DiAngelo will then bring you into the picture. No one else in the department will try to contact you, as no one else will be aware of this arrangement. Should someone from the department try to contact you, do not respond, but immediately call the lieutenant or the sergeant."

Ms Norah Jones now signed all of the papers acknowledging her acceptance of the conditions.

Welling closed the meeting by exchanging all of Elaine's ID and credit cards with temporary new ones issued to Norah Jones. Once she had changed her appearance, via her "Superman" schtick, without the need for a telephone booth (which at any rate, is hard to find in this cellular world), new photo IDs would be provided.

Without the need to exchange another word, Connie escorted Elaine from Welling's office, through the lobby to his car and to her soon-to-be-abandoned apartment.

CHAPTER 23

After a short limo trip to the private garage entry at her new residence, Alex escorted her to the elevator. With but two apartments on each floor and hers alone on the top, there was generally not much in the way of traffic in the building and absolutely none during the elevator ride to the penthouse.

Further protection was offered by the need for a special elevator key just to reach the top floor.

On the ride up, Alex filled Elaine in on how her new life was to be conducted until all outstanding "issues" had been resolved. A rotating member of his team of security agents would be posted 24/7 outside of her apartment entrance. None of them would be privy to her true identity. Someone would be on duty at the apartment even when she was out. All deliveries would be accepted by an agent in the garage. An agent would accompany the daily maid (whose security clearance had been provided in advance) during all of her chores. All visitors would be carefully pre-screened prior to admittance. The list went on, covering all anticipated possibilities of non-secure access to her apartment and her being.

Random contact was not acceptable.

The elevator door opened directly into an anteroom that was part of her apartment, but during her occupancy was for the use of the agent(s) on duty. A numbered keypad allowed entry into the rest of the apartment. At 9,000 square feet, the apartment dwarfed most freestanding homes in the world. Once inside, the word "apartment" seemed to be a misnomer.

Estate—sans land—was more appropriate. With luxurious decoration to match.

It had been custom decorated by Welling, et al several years ago when they had a case that required similar security. After the case had been closed, the apartment was used for very special visiting clients and as an occasional in-town convenience for senior partners. Very minor alterations had to be made to accommodate Elaine. For example, the Chihuly chandelier and Barbara Gray's paintings had already been transferred from Enrico's apartment to this one, after the detour for the paintings at the Metropolitan Museum of Art.

These were touches of much needed familiarity.

Additionally, the bedroom closet was now stocked with clothing, all Elaine's size, but definitely not in the style she would have worn. They were generally more colorful with bolder prints, shorter skirts and much more expensive fabrics. The designer names on the labels were well known around the world. The many pairs of shoes added at least two or three inches to her height, and bore designs and names that she used to gawk at in her copy of *Vogue*. Needless to say, all of the requisite accessories were laid out in their respective drawers.

Everything, and that included everything, that would be needed was there.

The king-sized bathroom, which was as big as her old bedroom, had all of the promised materials required to change her appearance, laid out on the counter. The walk-in shower was as big as most traditional bedrooms. Have you ever seen an Olympic-sized spa tub? It only lacked passing lanes.

The Emperor-sized master bedroom had many of her immediately needed personal effects, such as medications, librettos, personal diary, all displayed on the bed. What words could be used to describe the surroundings.

What was larger than Emperor-sized?

Each room was decorated in an expensive and very tasteful manner.

The entire 9,000 square feet of living space was surrounded by a twelve-foot-deep terrace with a 360-degree view of the City of New York. The west side had an uninterrupted view of her "private" park. The uninitiated call it Central Park. The Metropolitan Museum of Art was almost directly below her. The Hudson River with New Jersey on the other side were like neighbors. The south terrace had a direct view of the Battery area and all of the on-going reconstruction resulting from the 9/11 horror.

The Statue of Liberty was the centerpiece.

The view from the east terrace framed the East River with gentrifying Brooklyn on the opposite bank. Finally, the north terrace overlooked similar high-rise buildings melding into Harlem with the Bronx, Westchester and even Connecticut just beyond.

Elaine walked around the terrace twice because she just could not believe her eyes. Even after living in Manhattan for several years, the only time she had ever seen these types of views were in the movies. Now they were there just for her.

The rest of the afternoon was taken up with a detailed inspection of the apartment, room by room, closet by closet and drawer by drawer. All essentials had been taken into account and provided, and where necessary, customized for her use.

What she could not see was the roof area above the apartment where pressure plates and cameras were placed to detect unauthorized access. Any anomaly was immediately transmitted to the control room of the agent on duty.

Elaine's safety was paramount.

Nothing was left to chance.

CHAPTER 24

"The dude with the big-assed bass fiddle case was caught at least six times on surveillance cameras. Twice in the garage, twice in the elevator from the garage and twice on the primary elevator to the resident floors. Domestic face recognition files showed zilch. But, and this is a big BUT, Interpol files had at least 11 matching facial points! Enough to establish a definite identification."

Watkins went on, "Despite the red beard and wig and the drugstore glasses, there is no doubt that the perp is the man wanted in at least 12 countries as a professional assassin! We now know a lot about him, except his real name. There are at least 19 names listed by Interpol, none of them, with one exception, lead to any record or history. They lead us nowhere.

Nada.

The lone exception is the name Anthony Scalioni. There was an Anthony Scalioni in the US Army records as a trained sniper with the Green Berets between 1981 and 1989, at which time he was honorably discharged. He had been promoted to Staff Sergeant and acquired many commendations including a Silver Star and Purple Heart. There is some inconclusive evidence that he may have gone on to work for some US Government group, but that requires further checking. We need to get some Federal clearances to probe into Agency records.

I know what you are about to say, Connie, so I will follow up on this lead by locating his former army buddies as well as getting the necessary

Edward Gray

clearances to see if there was any connection with the obvious agencies that could have used his unique talents, like the FBI, CIA, Border Patrol, etc. I'm out of here."

"Good work Watkins! Our first solid lead."

Connie continued, "Bailey, I want you to check car rental agencies to see what you can dig up regarding credit card, driver's license and addresses that may have been used, and any other info that you can find. Also, check out where he got the rolling case for the contra bass. He obviously doesn't carry one with him just in case the need comes up. Check music shops, pawnshops and ads that may have been placed in local papers, trade magazines and online prior to the murder.

Why are you still sitting in front of me?

Move!

Everybody keep me informed as info develops. The Mayor and the Commissioner keep reminding me that results are needed . . . now.

We meet back here tomorrow at the same time.

Go.

Franco and Ozzie, hang around a sec."

After the others left, Connie told Ozzie to sit tight while he and Franco went to a private conference room and turned off all monitoring devices.

"Franco there is something I have to confide in you that must go no further than the space between my lips and your ears. What I am about to tell you has been cleared for our discussion by those previously read into it. You are to be brought into this strictly confidential information as my deputy with authorization to act on my behalf should I become incapacitated or otherwise unavailable."

Connie went on to describe the overall situation surrounding Ms Norah Jones and that when he was not otherwise engaged in pursuing his task force leads, he was to spend time overviewing her security arrangements and as her liaison with the department.

An awed Franco said, "Sure, boss, I will not take this responsibility lightly."

After Franco scooted off to introduce himself to Norah Jones, Connie called Ozzie in and said, "There is one angle we have not yet sufficiently considered and I want you to follow up on it. The victim is of Italian descent, as I am. I know that I am not in any way connected to "The

Family," but we must not neglect the possibility that Enrico may have had some sort of connection. Ozzie, I want you to dig into possible nefarious business connections in Indianapolis, as well as his family history. How did his dad build up one of the largest retail establishments in that city? Where did the money come from? Also see if you can pull up records that go back to his father's pre-immigration hometown and activities. The last name sounds like it's from southern Italy, perhaps even Sicily."

CHAPTER 25

Ozzie started with a telephone call to the City of Indianapolis, Records Division. After establishing his bona fides with the city clerk, he raised the pertinent questions regarding the establishment of the Indianapolis Department Store, including Title, ownership shares, sources of financing, banking history, debts not related to the original financing, etc.

"Detective, this will take several days to gather. Where can I reach you?"

Ozzie gave the clerk his cell phone number and reminded her that this was an urgent, high profile investigation. "I needed that info yesterday, but the end of the day today will be acceptable."

"Yes, sir," she responded. "I will do my best, and then some."

Ozzie embarked on a marathon of phone calls.

His first call was to Federated Department Stores, the new owners of the business. After three or four false leads, he was finally transferred to the right cubbyhole for the needed information.

He explained his quest, the urgency behind it, and asked that copies of all pertinent papers be e-mailed to him before the end of the day. The request covered the obvious information required to continue his investigation, items such as sales price, Payee(s), Title transfer info, continuing financial and other obligations to the seller(s), etc.

Ozzie's next call was to the editor of the *Indianapolis Sun*. He asked if she could assign someone to go over the paper's "morgue" files of issues of the paper dating back to the original establishment of the store, as well as its owner (prior to the sale to "Federated"), and e-mail copies of all pertinent articles to him. Again, the need for expediency in this task was explained.

His last call was to the Indianapolis Police Department, where he spoke to Assistant Chief Derrick Miller. Miller was well aware of the murder in New York of one of Indianapolis's very prominent former citizens. "He was a well-known resident who gave freely of his time and money to so many worthy causes."

Miller further said, "I will have someone check into the department records to see if there was anything that might prove to be helpful in your investigation."

When speaking to a fellow professional, it wasn't necessary to detail what was needed.

Ozzie leaned back on his much too hard desk chair, centered his muscular rear end, and pondered his next moves. Cerebral that is, without having to move his tush again.

Well, maybe one more time.

Tush immediately reminded Ozzie of touche, a coating that was somehow used by artists in creating lithographs. The important thing that jumped into his thought stream was not how it was used, but more specifically of the artist and her work.

Back to Google and the art of Barbara Gray.

Remember her? She was the artist responsible for the paintings in the victim's apartment. The ones Franco had sent to the Metropolitan Museum for inspection. Time to have them center their collective tushes and come up with a report.

Ozzie immediately called Franco to suggest follow-up while he was busy in Indianapolis.

It took Franco 14 1/2 minutes to get to the Met Museum and park his car. "No Parking Here" was meaningless when he was on official business —even sometimes as a perk when he was on a pleasure trip.

He entered the museum through the smaller side door in the south wing. This was an employee entrance and was located relatively close to the studios of the "Art Restoration and Conservation Group." They were the ones now entrusted with the inspection and X-ray analysis of the two Grays.

All of the prior dealings with the Director of this group, a Dr. Jill Pratzon, had been with Ozzie, so it was now necessary for Franco to present his credentials before gaining admittance to this very secure area. At any given time, there are hundreds of millions of dollars in Masters paintings awaiting certification of their provenance, and if necessary, an expert touch-up, before being hung for the public to view.

He was escorted to Studio A, passing old friends like Rembrandt, Monet, Rubens and others, long gone, but who continue to haunt one's esthetic values. Franco had never been into modern art but couldn't help but think, "Will Gray be among those names 100 years from now?"

Enough musing. On to work.

"So nice to put a face to the voice, Dr. Pratzon. I wanted to stop by and see firsthand what information you may have gleaned from the two Gray paintings being examined on our behalf."

"Detective, your timing is perfect. We have just finished an X-ray analysis and found some script in an under layer of "The Blue Nile." It was painted in Italian, and reads,

> "*Per accettare le vare origini del proprietario di questo quadro, e importante mettere in relazione le vicende segretamente documentata di re Vittorio Emanuele 1, con Don Correzzo di borgo di Corezzo di Marno*".

Fortunately, because of the prevalence of Italian Masters in the museum's collection, our business requires a mastery of the Italian language as a necessity. We often have to read Deeds of Provenance, old history books, sales records, etc., in Italian to ascertain the origin of the painting.

This one is easy to translate as it is written in modern Italian.

The literal meaning of what was written is:

> "To certify the true origins of the owner of this painting it is important to correlate the actions of King Victor Emanuel I with the town of Corezzo de Marno."

She continued, "Our investigation also determined that both paintings were done within the last seven years."

Franco thanked Dr. Pratzon for the valuable information and asked if she could find the address and phone number of the artist.

Dr. Pratzon indicated that Barbara Gray was well known to the Met, indeed several of her earlier works were currently on display in their third-floor contemporary collection. She checked her file and gave him the pertinent information. Fortunately, Gray's studio was located at the Brooklyn end of the Williamsburg Bridge, just a thirty-minute ride from the Met. If he had cause to use his siren, he could do it in fifteen minutes.

A quick call found Gray in her studio and, yes, she would be able to see Franco in the requested thirty minutes. As per procedure, Franco made a second call to the Precinct squad secretary to record his next move.

The building was a 1920's-era six-story whitish brick factory/warehouse that had been converted to artists' studios. With rooms housing one or two artists each, and about 30 rooms per floor, there had to be well over 200 artists using the facilities.

Some of them could even afford the rent.

A blond, longish haired, lanky young man with paint spattered jeans and a matching red and yellow checked flannel shirt, also enhanced by the same family of paint colors, was in the building entryway washing some brushes. Franco asked him if he knew which studio was Barbara Gray's.

"Fourth floor, second door on the right. No room numbers on any of the doors. The stairs are at the far end of this corridor. I would suggest the elevator, but it has not been working for at least the two years I have been here."

Franco's 5'9", 190-pound body was not made for four double flights of stairs. He mused, "If that damned gym at the precinct kept the Lieutenant in such great shape perhaps I should at least go look at it one day."

An unfulfilled promise he made to himself at least once a week.

Before opening the fire-door leading from the steps to the fourth floor, he wiped the sweat from his brow and waited a couple of minutes for his heart rate to come down to something approaching normal.

His knocking on the second door on the right was acknowledged with a lyrical, "Enter." It could only be Barbara Gray leaning over the massive canvas on the floor. Franco knew this because the lovely unfinished canvas

Murder at the Met

being worked on was similar in beauty, energy, swirling brush strokes and colors to that of the "Nile" series. The artist in front of him was quite beautiful and charming to boot.

"Hi, I'm Barbara Gray. Are you in the right studio?"

"Yes, Ms Gray! I am Sergeant Franco D'Angelo of the New York Police Department." He flashed his credentials. "I called earlier, and came down here to speak to you about an investigation we are pursuing."

"I don't know what help I can possibly provide. I don't even know what it is you are investigating. Is it a big deal crime?"

"Yes ma'am, we are investigating the murder of one Enrico Calzoni. As you may have read, he was murdered two weeks ago and found hanging at the Metropolitan Opera."

Barbara said, "I specifically remember that poor man's demise because, as I recall, he had two of my paintings in his art collection. You see I had never met the gentleman. Everything was arranged by a third party. That is, the purchase, the delivery and the payment."

"Ms Gray could you walk me through that, step by step and very slowly. Do not leave out any details even if they seem insignificant to you."

Barbara Gray continued, "Detective DiAngelo, do I have the name right?"

"Yes, go on."

"As I best remember, and the circumstances are hard to forget, about the end of June or July seven years ago, a man knocked on my studio door, just as you did a few moments ago. Wait a minute, it was the end of June because I remember having to go gift shopping for my husband's birthday. At any rate, I had never seen this gentleman before and he introduced himself as Claudio Cardini Giocci.

He was a well-dressed man in his 50's, about 5'11" tall, carrying about 180 pounds of well-developed muscles and had a thick Italian accent."

Franco interrupted, "What about hair, eye color, scars and other distinguishing features?"

She continued, "As an artist I can usually remember people I have seen in great detail. Mr. Giocci had a full head of wavy black hair, no facial hair, black eyes, no visible scars, no limp or other distinguishing features. If you like I could easily sketch his face before you leave, but please first tell me what this is all about."

"Ms Gray, of course you should know why I am here and asking so many questions. Do you recall the details, as reported in the media some three weeks ago about the still unresolved murder of Mr. Enrico Calzoni, that I had just mentioned?"

"Of course I do. As I said he was the gentleman to whom my paintings were shipped, at the request of Mr. Giocci. I remember his telling me at the time that the paintings were to be an important gift for his favorite cousin.

It was particularly memorable because of the strange circumstances surrounding the request. I had the images of the as yet undone pieces in my mind, but not on canvas, which, strangely, he wanted to supply. Not only supply the canvas, but pre-stretched and primed with gesso. I have always done the latter by myself, but he insisted that he supply it. He claimed that it was necessary because of certain climatic conditions that they would ultimately have to face. He assured me that the stretched canvases would be perfectly acceptable to my demanding requirements.

I of course accepted his conditions as long as the canvases met said conditions, such as use of linen vs traditional cotton canvas, flat application of the gesso, no raw spots, and finally, diagonally-braced hardwood frames that could be broken down for transportation.

He then opened his briefcase, put $100,000, in cash, on the table and said that the remaining half was guaranteed and would be paid in the same manner upon shipment.

Yes, officer, that is my usual price for two large canvases, but never in advance, especially of an as yet undone work. He assured me that whatever was on the canvases would be more than acceptable because he and his cousin were great admirers of my work."

She continued, "After the final payment, the completed works were to be sent directly to his cousin, one Enrico Calzoni. The paintings were finished two months later, and after they dried (acrylic paint, which I exclusively use, dries in a matter of hours), they were crated and shipped to Mr. Calzoni, and the remaining payment made by a Western Union money order.

I never heard anything further from either gentleman.

Now please tell me why my paintings are so important to your investigation."

Franco responded with, "Please bear with me for just one more question, and then I will fill you in. Was the gesso on the canvases particularly thick? Did you notice anything under the gesso?"

Ms Gray said, "The gesso underlay seemed to be thicker on one of them, but I thought it was to cover the wavy dirt lines that were apparently on the canvas. Canvas is occasionally soiled in shipment."

"You have been extremely cooperative and I promised that I would fill you in after you answered the last two questions, and will now do so."

He then explained about the work that had been done by the Metropolitan Museum of Art labs, and their results.

Ms Gray turned ashen white, which was actually quite attractive given her soft brown hair and large dark brown eyes. Unfortunately, this time those dark, penetrating eyes conveyed a picture of absolute confusion.

Franco then rapid-fired the obvious questions, "Do you have any contact info for Mr. Giocci? Has he ever contacted you again? Who made the shipping arrangements? Did he leave a business card? Did he leave any contact information?"

"Whoa, one question at a time. First let me get my tax return records for the year of the commission. They are stored in that metal filing cabinet in the corner, where all of my receipts and supporting info is stored."

She reached into the third drawer and pulled out a file with large black block letters on the front, "Tax – 2008."

Ms Gray shuffled through all of the stacked papers and after a few minutes pulled out four or five of them that pertained to that transaction.

"This one is the purchase agreement. Note that it has the cost, payment schedule and delivery details. The only address is that of Mr. Calzoni in Indianapolis, Indiana. The other papers relate to the tax implications of the sale and specific caveats, such as completion dates, image ownership, resale restrictions, etc."

Franco immediately put on latex gloves and placed the papers in a plastic evidence sleeve.

He explained that although there were likely to be a number of fingerprints on the sheets, there was a remote possibility that the forensics lab would be able to identify Mr Giocci's by process of elimination of those that could be identified.

Just a possibility.

He asked Ms Gray to stop by the local police station to be fingerprinted so that they would know which were hers when found on the canvases and the papers he now had in the evidence sleeve.

He then gave Ms Gray a release form that declared that the papers would be returned to her at the conclusion of the investigation. He also gave her his contact card should she need to speak to him about anything else she could think of, or with other related questions.

Franco thanked Ms Gray for her time and for being so cooperative and headed back to the Precinct.

CHAPTER 26

Connie had been staring at the pictures pinned to the left side of the massive cork board on the east wall of the squad room for two and a half eternities before the eyeballs moved three feet further east and refocused on the time frame that covered significant events/discoveries since the first call to the precinct two weeks ago.

He was not looking at what was there, but at what was missing. He mentally noted that Franco had not reported back regarding that artist Ozzie had delegated him to chase down. There were no reports from Watkins and Carol regarding GosChem, and the unauthorized disbursements of their rigorously controlled sodium penta-foliate anesthetic. Where was Ozzie's report on the victim's business activities?

He needed another meeting of the squad ASAP and asked Donna, the group secretary, to get everyone who was readily available, back to the squad room at seven the nect morning.

"All right, boys and girls, finish your bagels without spilling your lattes and let's get this Show-and-Tell Party going."

Bagels and lattes? That would be almost as unacceptable in NYC as mayonnaise on a pastrami sandwich!

"Franco, why don't you lead off and tell us what you have learned."

Connie usually started these meetings with Franco because he could depend on his having some really significant info, and setting the tone for the others.

Franco did not disappoint. He told the group about the Museum's findings under the paintings and his subsequent visit to the artist. He also indicated that he had left the artist's studio with her quick sketch of the mysterious Mr. Giocci.

"The forensics lab is following up on the fingerprints found on the papers I received from Ms Gray as well as with a "Facial Characteristics Recognition" scan, based on the sketch she provided me with. As soon as the results are known, I will fill you in and follow up, as appropriate."

Ozzie was on deck next.

He indicated that there were some interesting anomalies that he had noted regarding the deceased's past business ownership activities. A trip to Indianapolis was definitely a necessity in order to dig deeper, and it would be necessary to do some further archival digging in Italy. Franco's findings seemed to agree with this approach.

Unrelenting international press coverage of this bizarre murder put unwanted attention on their investigation. It took just a few hours to get the Chief on board with his agreement to release special funds to cover the overseas travel.

Connie then split the effort, with Ozzie heading out once again to Indianapolis and Franco, because of his almost Italian language ability, going to Italy.

CHAPTER 27

Buffeting winds in the early evening hours made the landing more than uncomfortable. You know the feeling, clenched knuckles, any remaining color drained from the face, eyes bulging and stomach ready to heave. We have all experienced it.

Well at least I have.

Ozzie had faced worse in his life.

As stoic a being as he was, he still found it hard to subsist on a dinner of water and peanuts, as so elegantly presented in cattle class, with that miserable landing served as dessert.

Ozzie was basically a good guy, so it could not be considered his "Just Dessert"!

Before leaving the plane, he retrieved his gun from the Captain and with a backpack containing all his needs for the trip, bypassed the baggage area and went directly to the Avis counter. After picking up a plain black Ford sedan, which immediately marked him as a cop, he drove directly to the Marriott Courtyard on Ohio Boulevard, two blocks from Indianapolis Police Headquarters.

A courtesy upgrade to the concierge level had been arranged by his Indianapolis police hosts. The suite was much larger and better furnished than his own small apartment on Montgomery Street in Brooklyn.

After an almost real dinner at Friday's, on the next block, he went back to the hotel and crashed for the night. Tomorrow was going to be an exhausting day.

Promptly at seven the next morning, a rejuvenated Ozzie once again presented himself to the admissions officer at Indianapolis Central Police Headquarters. He was told that he was expected by Lt. Jenoff in conference room 263.

At 5'4" and carrying about 280 pounds, Alex Jenoff was not exactly built like the former "Governator" of California. Fortunately, most of that weight was probably composed of brain matter. He was one hell of a smart detective and had earned the respect of all who worked with him.

After about 2.6 minutes of small talk, Jenoff presented the information that their two days of paperwork had uncovered since Ozzie's last trip.

"We had a team checking for the background info you requested and also dug up the morgue data (yep, another intended pun) you wanted. I suggest we go over all of the above step by step and see where you want to go from there.

It would make sense to discuss the historical newspaper background first and then present what we found in our investigation."

Early copies of *The Daily Herald*, dating back to 1933, listed the name of Pietro Calzoni as a new arrival to Indianapolis in the "Welcome to New Neighbors" column. According to the short bio, "Pietro has moved his family from their home in NYC to our fair city in order to establish a personal dry goods business during these very difficult depression years."

In October 1949, the paper had a feature article applauding the growth of the Calzoni family enterprise. It described how after years of growth, starting with door-to-door sales of household linens and other dry goods, in 1939 he was finally able to open a small brick and mortar shop on Evan Boulevard. His inventory had expanded to include men's haberdashery items and a corner featuring ladies high fashion garments. All of this in a space that was only slightly larger than the corner newspaper store.

The real thrust of the article was how he had parlayed his micro shop into the Indianapolis Department Store, a three-story, half-a-city-block-long, major addition to the city's retail needs. The ribbon was cut by Mayor O'Brien, with the entire City Council and other honored guests in attendance. Free wine and snacks from the store's food hall was distributed to the entire crowd of onlookers.

Nowhere did the article report how this major undertaking was financed.

Nowhere did the article report who served as officers or board members of the enterprise.

Nowhere did the article report on if and when the construction was granted permits by the city.

Nowhere did the article report on how the construction contract was awarded.

Jenoff said how the "nowhere"s bothered him, so he dug deeper.

He combed through City Hall building permits, and could not find any issued before construction commenced, not even after the fact.

Nada.

He then checked construction progress inspection reports. Reports were issued on a timely basis throughout the construction period. He was given high marks for everything being done. This did not feel right, as comparable reports during the same period on other major construction sites showed multiple violations of building codes that had to be rectified.

What was wrong with this picture?

Subsequent news items over the next few years reported the early retirement of Mayor O'Brien and his new trophy wife to a recently purchased major estate in Palm Beach, Florida. A check of his tax records, which were in the public domain because of his government position, showed that he did not have a pot to you know what, throughout his entire working life.

So where did the money to purchase the estate suddenly come from?

Although on a lesser scale, similar retirements to better "living conditions" were noted for various city inspectors and other petty officials associated with the construction of the new store.

It was patently obvious where their newfound wealth came from, but a direct link to the owner of the store would be more difficult to prove.

Jenoff dug deeper into the bank records of Pietro Calzoni and found infusions of large sums of money into his bank account as were needed during the construction, and subsequently, when the store had to be stocked with merchandise. Bank records indicated that the funds came from the New York Federation of Sanitation and Security Workers.

Jenoff said to Ozzie, "This is where my investigation into the early days

Edward Gray

of the store ends. It is now up to you to follow the money trail in New York City. I will continue probing into the recent year's sale of the property and Enrico Calzoni's finances. Will let you know if anything pops up."

After a great dinner at Fleming's Steakhouse to thank Jenoff for his efforts, Ozzie caught the late flight back to JFK.

With the aroma of the filet mignon still wafting from his jacket, United Airlines peanuts were heartily rejected with a smile.

CHAPTER 28

Unlike Ozzie, Franco was a born flyer, always infatuated with airline travel, but seldom able to afford long trips on his minimal NYC police detective's income. The assignment to follow up in Italy was destined to be a beautiful adventure.

The eight-hour flight from New York's JFK Airport landed at Rome's Fiumicino Airport at 8:30 am and was all he had hoped for. Even the hot dinner that Alitalia served in coach was better than he had expected. The lasagna was not quite what his late mother could whip up (in under ten hours of simmering sauces, in a small hot kitchen), but was quite acceptable.

The one-hour bus ride from the airport to the center of Rome was followed by a twenty-minute cab ride that brought him to his hotel near the central Nationala Policia station, just off the Via Nazionale. He checked into the hotel early and walked the few blocks to the station, stopping on the way for a morning espresso and warm roll.

After identifying himself to the Admissions Commissaire, he was escorted to the second-floor office of Commodore Laticco, Chief of Detectives for the City of Rome. As Franco soon found out, the Commodore was also quite influential and well known in investigations throughout Italy.

He was the "go to" man when all else failed.

Laticco's English was quite good. Franco's Italian was quite bad, so

English prevailed. When the proper translation could not be understood, this being Italy, hand gestures filled the gap.

Communication proved to be excellent.

A cup of espresso immediately appeared as Franco sat down. It was the second of some 320,000 he would consume over the next three days.

After a few pleasantries, they got down to the reason for the trip.

"Your e-mail last Tuesday was what you Americans would call a "bombshell," for the department and certainly for Italy. The Prince is a very popular national figure. I immediately started our internal investigation and came up with the following.

Prince Emanuel's principal home is the Castello Ponte Nuovo just seven kilometers south of Milan. On 112 acres, inclusive of the town of Ponte Nuovo, his small "cabin" has 97 rooms serviced by a permanent household staff of 22. It is not too shabby a place to live in. However, he still manages to spend most of his time in either his apartment on the Via Condola here in Rome or in mid-winter in his ski "shack" in the alpine village of Cervinia. There he spends most of each morning just looking at the majestic Matterhorn and planning the rest of the day.

My family of five could very comfortably live in the servant's quarters of any of them.

Add to the above his royal stature and enormous wealth, coupled with his popularity from an adoring public, and he will be a very difficult suspect to go after. Questions?"

Franco tried to take this all in, and finally responded with, "The questions are obvious, it's the answers that I need. I need to know about the Prince's personal finances in great detail, especially if there are any hidden financial problems. I need to know about his security team: who they are, how they operate, their global contacts, their domestic and international movements, political and police contacts, etc.

I need to know how and where we contact him, especially if there is any governmental protocol that must be followed because of his position.

If it can be determined that he is directly involved, I need to know who has jurisdiction in a case of murder in the USA where an Italian Prince is the prime suspect.

Those are only the opening questions that must be answered. The rest will evolve as we dig deeper."

Laticco had enough years in the business that nothing ever really rattled him. The last two minutes of Franco's soliloquy caused him to sit back and reflect. That was about as close to being fazed as he ever got.

"If the Prince were a grade "A" bastard," responded Lattico, "there would be minimal problems, as the people of Italy would not object. Indeed, they would support the eviction and prosecution of him. However, the Prince is a prince of a person, the son of the late King Emanuel who was much revered by the public. He is not a Berlusconi type so there will be much resistance and public outcry.

We will have many obstacles in our investigation path.

I must leave you for several days while I consult with my superiors in the Department and most certainly in the Government political and protocol groups. This will all be done on a confidential basis to minimize the chance for word to get to the Prince too early in our investigation. But regardless, even with all the warnings for the necessity of secrecy, the Prince will be aware of all within hours.

Go enjoy the eternal beauty of Rome until I get back to you."

After many a thank you, Franco took the long walking route back to his hotel. At only 11:00 am in Rome, it was much too early in NY to call Rico at the Precinct. The city map supplied to Franco by the hotel concierge highlighted all of the historic sites he had known since childhood, only for him, through picture books. He had about three hours to joyfully waste, on:

The Pantheon
chocolate gelato
the Colosseum
limoncello gelato
the Forum
fettuccine amatriciana
the Vatican
pepperoni pizza
Trevi Fountain
veal scallopini scarpiello
the Roman aqueduct
strawberry gelato

Why continue the list when three hours would be enough time to only make a small dent in it?

Too little time for too many things.

As an experienced detective, he first analyzed his tourist leads, I mean needs, in a logical order of priority, assigned time slots, and only then jumped into action.

Because of his heritage, coupled with his strong sense of Italo/Roman history, it was natural for Franco to address the most important need first:

chocolate gelato from the fabled Gelateria Doney on the Via Veneto.

History could wait another few minutes, and it did.

As the last few drops of chocolate paradise dripped on his shirtsleeve, Franco's eyes wandered over to the kiosk on his left and zeroed in on a headline in one of the Roman tabloid newspapers, with a familiar picture. One Euro later, he read the story about the Prince's latest donation to the improvement of life in Rome. He had given 10,000 Euro to the ISPCA (Italian Sociatia Preventura etc.) specifically for the feeding of stray cats in the capital city. A favorite charity of the city dwellers.

The picture showed the Prince, in his home, handing a check to some unidentified representative of the charity.

The picture was undated.

The recipient was not identified.

The Prince looked younger than in photos he had just seen at the Precinct this morning.

The whole strange incident was properly noted and stored in the recesses of Franco, the detective's mind, as he strolled over to the Pantheon.

You know the place. Built about 100 years after JC walked on this planet, it still featured the largest dome ever built, with a great big hole in the middle. Sort of like an oversized bagel, with everything. Staring through the hole for some ten minutes gave Franco the opportunity to concentrate his thoughts, itemize what he wanted to discuss with Connie in the upcoming phone call to NYC and a proposed course of the investigation here in Rome.

The morning was far from wasted.

CHAPTER 29

Franco's leisurely yet simple lunch consisted of a toasted pancetta ham and provolone cheese sandwich, washed down by a glass of the house chianti and was completed to his absolute satisfaction with a dish of lemon gelato. It kept the mind and body in sync as he wended his way back through winding streets, masses of people, curbside stalls and toy-sized cars, back to his hotel.

If the gelato routine was maintained, he would likely have to pay an overweight "baggage" surcharge for the flight home.

Miraculously, the hotel was just where he remembered it should be. That was no small accomplishment in a city with streets as convoluted as in Rome. Ask three Romans where such-and-such street is and you will get four or five different answers. Remember, Franco was used to Manhattan where all of the streets are laid out in an almost perfect grid that every newcomer can easily master.

In the privacy of an empty corner in the hotel lounge, Franco called Connie on the secure cell phone provided to him by the department for this overseas trip. He did not dare place such a call from his hotel room, which may very well have been compromised.

"Hello, boss? Yes, I arrived in one piece, without my piece, as I came in peace and even received a loaner piece. A Glock, from my contact on the force here, Detective Laticco.

Don't get wise! That's the only piece I got in Rome—so far.

Speaking of that, how is our charge, beautiful Ms Jones doing? Tell her I miss her!"

"She is being well taken care of," was Connie's terse response.

He then filled Connie in on the meeting, especially noting that in accordance with Italian law, only official Italian Governmental groups could conduct investigations on Italian soil. Franco would be permitted to accompany the assigned team and offer advice, but only as a consultant.

"What's my next move, boss? Do I stay here and see this through or do I hop on the next plane back to the big city?"

Connie did not respond immediately, and finally said, "It would serve our purposes best if you stayed there for a while and ensured that their investigation is not shoved under the carpet by certain people with influence. In the meantime, I will have the Chief contact our State Department and determine how they feel about the stated investigative limits. We will also try to ensure that our Embassy is aware of your presence and prepared to support you.

I want daily reports on your progress. Limit them to your secure phone, or directly via the Embassy. I don't trust the internet.

Also, fatso, you forgot to add a limoncello aperitif to your Italian Bucket-List!

Ciao."

The rest of the day was continued with his second list of "to-do" items, but this time, work-related research was interspersed. After all, gelato was not the only reason he was in Italy.

The day continued with a visit to the Forum, including the mandatory photo with the shoddily costumed "Roman Gladiator." Well worth the three Euro to prove that he really was there.

On to Plaza Monteleone for dinner.

The Caprese salad (tomato and mozzarella slices with drizzled oil and oregano) followed by fettuccine amatriciana (wide pasta covered with a sauce simmered for hours with tomatoes, pancetta ham, onions, spices and love.) The meal was accompanied by his favorite Chianti Reserva wine. The dinner was beautifully capped with, of course, vanilla gelato.

"Perfecto."

He felt like he had at last come home to the grandma's simple cottage, one that he had always dreamt of but had never actually known. His real grandmother was an American born physician and in reality, a lousy cook except, for some reason unknown to him, her lasagna. It was probably store bought.

Even her tea tasted burnt.

So much for his Italian heritage.

After a stroll around the Plaza, back to the hotel for a jet lag induced and absolutely needed, full night's sleep. The memory of events between taking off his shoes and the 6:00 am alarm the next morning was almost a complete blank. Almost is the operative word as there were interrupting visions of gelato and Elaine.

Whoa, how did Elaine sneak into his subliminal thoughts?

CHAPTER 30

Laticco and Franco sat across the conference room table from several other people. Their faces were those of Italian Government boldface names that were familiar, but obviously, he had never had the opportunity to actually meet. The tall gray haired, with beard to match, individual was introduced as the Commissioner of Police. Next to him were high-ranking representatives of the State Police, the Interior Ministry and the Ministry of Foreign Affairs.

The Italian Government had been contacted the day before, late in the afternoon, by the US Embassy and was obviously taking this affair very seriously.

Fortunately, all spoke reasonable English so that Franco did not have to embarrass himself with his "kindergarten" Italian.

He gave a twenty-minute briefing on what had been learned, how they had determined the Prince's involvement and where the US investigation was headed. He was particularly protective of his new friend Elaine's new identity and location, neither of which was shared with them.

By the time he had finished detailing the investigation background, Franco had polished off his third cup of espresso. Not quite used to a drink that you could almost eat with a fork, he was, to say the least, quite alert.

Alert-and-a-half was more like it.

A scoop of raspberry gelato at this point would have been appreciated.

The next hour was spent in answering questions and charting a course to be pursued by the Italian authorities. It was made quite clear to Franco that he was there only as an observer and consultant with no active investigative input. This had been agreed to by the US Embassy and the Italian Government. They even asked for the return of the loaner Glock sidearm to underscore the limitation on his role.

It was then made perfectly clear by the Foreign Minister's representative that this investigation was to be absolutely confidential to those in the room and the investigative team.

"Should this be leaked prematurely, the Prince will take any defensive action available to him, including rousing the public to protest what he would categorize as an "American Witch Hunt." We are too well aware of his popularity and the polarization that could cause.

Is that understood?

Detective Commodore Laticco, you are hereby granted the authority to lead this investigation on behalf of all of the agencies involved. You are to restrict all current and derived information to your select core team on a confidential basis and report directly to the Commissioner. All other superiors and colleagues will be informed that you are on special assignment for the Bureau of Tourism. That would help to explain the American's presence in your squad room."

The others left, leaving just Franco and Laticco to do what had to be done.

Do what had to be done. What an understatement.

What had to be done was to investigate one of the most popular public figures in Italy in complete secrecy and prove that he was somehow complicit in the murder of someone he had never met, some 6,000 miles away. Further, this was to be done with a police task force that could not even tell their wives and/or mistresses what they were doing.

Laticco and Franco spent the rest of the day and evening through a dinner that ended with, surprise, strawberry gelato. Their discussion continued over multiple glasses of Grappa well into the wee hours as they charted out the needs and forward course of the investigation. Laticco now had to determine how much staff would be needed, who they were to be and then bring them on board, post haste.

The next critical item to be addressed was the need for a secure office away from Headquarters.

Early the next morning, Lattico placed a few calls and found an available large room within the Ministry of Tourism's building on the Via dei Fori Imperiali—an excellent choice that reinforced their tourism cover story. To Franco's amazement the next day, it was exactly where Laticco told him it would be, just three meandering blocks south of the Colosseum. Their assigned area was in the under-utilized Greenland Affairs Division, a group without staff or budget, but with decent space set apart from the busier areas of the building. A few more calls arranged for the immediate delivery and setup of office furniture, telephones, office supplies, etc.

That took the rest of the next day.

More sightseeing for Franco. In between the Vatican and the Trevi Fountain (and a small cup of mango gelato for energy) he scheduled a visit to the US Embassy on Capitoline Hill.

Ambassador Douglas Cronin, one of a rare breed of career diplomats appointed to a major ambassadorial position, was very professional and filled Franco in on his limitations while on Italian soil. He then called in the Embassy's Manager of Forest Conservation, Stan Levine, whose other responsibility happened to be CIA Station Chief. Stan and Franco then withdrew to the Embassy safe room for a more detailed conversation.

After presenting the case's background and its possible international repercussions, they agreed on a joint course of action. Franco would continue his liaison role with Laticco and would keep Stan informed on a daily basis as to progress, or lack of same. Stan would provide whatever backup Franco might require as well as segregating him from enquiries by non-involved Italian Agencies, like immigration, customs, etc. Cell phone numbers were exchanged and Franco took his leave.

On the third day, the newly formed elite squad moved into their new quarters and were officially greeted by Laticco, who also used the occasion to introduce Franco.

The five additional detectives, a computer specialist and the squad secretary were sworn to secrecy under the terms of the Official Secrets Act. They were then told the ground rules and briefed on the case background by Laticco and Franco. All of them were painfully aware of the outrage that would break out should the public prematurely learn about the investigation of their dear Prince. This had to be avoided at all costs until absolute proof was found as to his connection to the affair, and official charges made.

As was required, this most select squad was not made privy to Elaine's new identity or whereabouts. Once again, Franco was extremely protective of his responsibility and special new friend.

An eight-foot-wide HD computer screen had been mounted on the north wall (to avoid direct sunlight from interfering with visibility) complete with photos of the Prince, advisors, close friends and his principal residences, all on the left half. The remaining screen space was to be filled in as the investigation developed.

Each of the individuals on the screen was identified by name with a brief bio and current location. Individual assignments were then made for coverage of all on the list by the various detectives, except for the Prince. He would be the personal responsibility of Laticco.

Laticco simply barked "Pronto," and all scurried off to their assignments.

Italy's Laticco and New York's Connie must have been twins separated at birth (and by mother), both ending staff presentations with "Get moving."

The rest of the afternoon was totally consumed in a strategy meeting to determine how, when and where the two of them would proceed with the Prince's investigation.

CHAPTER 31

The new Braun electric razor that Lucy had bought for Connie's birthday the week before was finally put to use on its test drive. Lo and behold, smooth without the usual morning patchwork of toilet paper on his face to stem the bleeding of razor nicks.

Ain't modern technology great! To conservative Connie, so set in his ways, this was a startling new invention, akin to cavemen using fire as a friend.

The rest of his morning routine was unchanged. Sleep-hangover with brain function now at 62.3%. Coffee and newspapers were still additional necessities to increase bodily function.

By the time he got to the office, the daily call from Franco informed him of the initial progress in Italy. This was followed up with Connie's daily call, on behalf of the otherwise busy overseas Franco, to the agent in charge of Elaine's security.

Now he desperately needed some progress in NYC, and it ultimately came via the unrelenting efforts of Ozzie. Follow up followed by follow up followed by—you get the picture—produced a path to the killer.

It resulted from his visit to GosChem Pharmaceuticals, two days ago. In poring through their invoices, he came across one that seemed somewhat strange. It was for a trial amount (10cc's) of the rare anesthetic found in Enrico's body by Dr. Hochschuler, the Medical Examiner. The strange part was the customer. It was sent to the Italo-American Medical Welfare Center in the Bronx.

His instinct immediately took over, as this institution was totally unknown to him, especially as he had been cruising the streets and alleyways of the five boroughs for many years. Further investigation on his part could not find it listed in any medical institution directory.

Back in the office he turned to the detective's second best friend (the Glock always came in first), the computer. He Googled "The Italo-American Medical Welfare Center" and found the following entry:

> *Established on August 7, 2008 as a medical resource for recent Italian immigrants to the United States who did not have any other medical coverage available to them. This free service was totally privately funded by Prince Emanuel II, heir to the now defunct throne of Italy.*
>
> *In his dedication address he envisioned that this institution would ease the pain and financial burden that illness could cause to the newcomer in his new country. He further provided a substantial sum of money to cover operating expenses in perpetuity.*
>
> *The prince currently serves as Chairman of the Board of Directors.*

Talk about a smoking gun!

That afternoon Ozzie drove to IAMWC (Italian American etc.) on the Bronx Concourse. The main drag, in this second largest borough was home to the largest population of Italian-Americans in the city.

The center was a two-story building that echoed the same red brick facade as the surrounding ones. The major difference was that this one was much newer and better maintained than its neighbors. It also had a steady stream of people seeking help. Regardless of any other motivation, the IAMWC appeared to be an important neighborhood institution.

Ozzie identified himself to the receptionist and asked to see Dr. Giovanni Fellah, Director of the Center, without delay. He purposely came with no advance warning so that the good doctor's answers to his questions would be spontaneous.

Within two minutes Ozzie was directed to Dr. Fellah's office. He entered just as an elderly woman, assisted by a cane, was leaving.

"Dr. Fellah, I am Detective Ozdjemti with the NYC Police Department Homicide Division. I am here to ask you some questions about an ongoing investigation that you could possibly shed some light on."

"This sounds important! Is it also ominous? Am I somehow involved? Do I need to worry about something I know nothing about? Do I have to go to the police station? Do I need a lawyer?"

Ozzie smiled, to put the Doctor at ease, and said, "Relax Doc, I just need some information." The good doctor was obviously not used to such a visit and was clearly nervous. Ozzie's well-developed second sense told him that Dr. Fellah was not guilty of anything other than watching too many crime shows on TV.

Ozzie went on, "I wanted to chat with you about something that arose the other day that perhaps you could help us with. We were checking the records of a pharmaceutical company and found something that piqued our curiosity. One of their shipments to your group was for some 10cc of sodium-penta-folinate, a rather rare coma-inducing drug. We were wondering if indeed your group was the recipient of this delivery and how it was used."

"Why, yes, I remember it well.

About three weeks ago I received a telephone call from Sgn. Arturo Freschi, Private Secretary to our Chairman, Prince Emanuel II. He told me in confidence that the Prince was going through a very difficult illness that was not being treated successfully with existing protocols.

The Prince's Medical Team was in contact with a research group at New York's Columbia Medical School doing advance work in this area with outstanding success and asked us to assist. They were planning to send one of their research physicians to Italy to lead the Prince's medical team in applying this new approach. The physician asked for us to obtain this particular medication for his use with the Prince. As a research doctor he was unable to obtain this drug that could only be shipped to hospitals.

I naturally ordered same and received it three days later."

Ozzie interrupted, "What did you do with it?"

"I Googled the Columbia Medical Research roster and found that there was indeed a Dr. Matthew Stinton at the facility, and called the private number provided to me by Sgn. Freschi. It was answered by Dr. Stinton, who arranged to pick it up that afternoon."

"Did you meet him?" asked Ozzie.

"Yes, I would not let such a medication be in the hands of a non-professional. He came to my office and we had a brief chat about the wellbeing of the Prince and how an induced coma would facilitate the curative treatment. He seemed to be quite expert in this new field."

Ozzie reached into his folder and removed a picture. "Would this be the Dr. Stinton that you met that day?"

"Why, yes, that certainly seems to look like him, but as I recall he had a red beard, red hair and glasses," Dr. Fellah replied.

"Bingo."

Ozzie replaced the picture of Anthony Scalioni, or whatever his real name was, back in the folder.

CHAPTER 32

Connie picked up his cell phone on the second ring and listened without interruption as Ozzie recounted his visit to the IAMWC and the revelations made by Dr. Fellah.

They were zeroing in on hard evidence. All they needed now was one Mr. Scalione. They also had to tie him to the Met on the day of the murder. It was toward this end that Connie was now seated in a backstage room normally used by the Maestro during pre-concert rehearsal discussions with soloists and First Seats.

"So, tell me again, Harry, what happened after you took up your post at the artist's entrance at 11:00 am on the day of the murder?"

"Well, sir, I relieved Ken of his responsibilities and took possession of the visitors' log book. As I had indicated, we record the names of all who pass through these doors."

Leafing through the pages, he came to the day etched in the memory of all in that revered building, and continued. "As you can see there were only three entries before noon. That is not at all unusual on performance days as most of the artists generally start to arrive about two hours prior to curtain up. As you may know, an evening performance was scheduled for that day. I have had this job for 12 years and two of them were well known to me as long-term Met orchestra members. Musicians do tend to come in from time to time at odd hours to change the strings or valves or make other adjustments to their instruments.

"That afternoon there was only one new artist gaining entry. As you can see from my record, it was the new bassist. Mr. Hendrik Steinflesch. He had been in a few days earlier and established his ID with Hank, who was on duty that day. I was sure it was him because I was aware of a newcomer from the log record. I also knew it was the new bassist because that was not a flute container he was schlepping."

"What time was that?"

Harry continued, "It was 3:20 pm. As you know there was no record of his departing because of the ensuing panic and lockdown. I assumed he left with the others after all of the emergency alarms went off."

"Now, once again, please describe his appearance to me."

"I have a pretty good memory for faces because of the requirements of my job. Mr. Steinflesch was indeed memorable because of his red beard, red hair and glasses."

Connie took the picture of Scalione out of his case and put it on the table in front of Harry.

"Yeah, that sure looks like him. I recognize the nose and ears and can easily visualize the beard, and glasses."

"Harry, many thanks, you have been a big help."

Connie then drove to his second appointment of the day, the late Enrico Calzoni's apartment building.

"No, Lieutenant, I was not on duty that day. Jaime was. He is in our staff room preparing to leave for the day. I'll get him out here for you."

Connie thanked the concierge and then greeted Jaime as he came out of the door behind the concierge stand. "I know that you have been questioned by our detectives regarding the recent murder of one of the tenants, but we have some new information that I wanted to see you about." Reaching into his case, Connie pulled out two photos and showed them to Jaime. One of them was of Joe Biden as a young man. The other was the one important to this case.

In broken English, Jaime indicated that he had never seen that first person. However, the second photo looked a little familiar except that the man with the big case that day had a red beard, etc.

Connie took out a red crayon and drew a beard and colored in the hair. With a black crayon, he drew in glasses.

"Si, that's him!"

Connie's friend Crayola Red paid off much like a slot machine, only better!

"Thank you, Jaime. If you are free, we will take an official statement at the station later today."

As far as Connie was concerned, this was the final link that tied Scalione in as the murderer. Now all they had to do was find him and a direct tie to the financier of the operation, Prince Emanuel II.

CHAPTER 33

There it was, the Smoking Gun.

This Smoking Gun was in the guise of a piece of paper within a huge stack of pieces of paper. This special one was a document found in the office of the Roman branch of the Prince's charities organization. An authorization, bearing the Prince's signature, for the transfer of $500,000 (Euro equivalent) to the Italo-American Medical Welfare Center for the purpose of hiring a prominent research physician, one Dr. Stinton. The purpose noted was "To investigate the effect of certain medications on the efficacy of neural stimulants." No further details were noted.

Let's back up for a minute.

The complicated discussions and subsequent negotiations involved Connie, the New York City Police Commissioner and Mayor, the US State Department, the Italian Embassy, the Italian Foreign Minister, the Italian Carabinieri Director and, finally, Laticco.

Each group involved had its own agenda and restrictions. After several days and all-nighters of face-to-face, telephone and e-mail discussions, nothing.

Finally, the Italian Prime Minister and the President of the US spoke to each other over secure phones and almost miraculously, convergence occurred.

The way forward was agreed upon.

A secret warrant was now issued by the Italian Foreign Ministry permitting Laticco's men to covertly enter the Prince's Rome quarters. They spent the better part of two nights poring through all of the papers on file until the eureka moment.

See Smoking Gun, above.

Basically, that was all they'd needed to gain authorization to get into a greater in-depth investigation of the Prince, even if it meant that his involvement could become public knowledge. That latter part was to be avoided, if possible, but for the time being they needed to dig up even more evidence of his direct role.

An absolute indictment was required to pursue a person of this stature. There was no room for suspicions, only substantiated facts.

A copy of the first major documented Proof of Crime was immediately and covertly transmitted to Connie via the US Embassy. This gave Connie's team the needed evidence to more openly investigate the New York office of the IAMWC.

However, the problem in Italy continued, as it was still necessary to obtain further direct evidence of the Prince's involvement in order to build a legal case for indictment and provide for this popular figure's extradition to the USA.

The second piece of damning evidence was dug up by the very diligent and time-consuming efforts on the part of one of Laticco's detectives. The officer spent several days combing through phone records of all of the Prince's residences and offices.

Some three months ago, there were a number of calls to a cellphone in the USA. The officer then contacted Connie in NYC and found that the number called was to the disposable cell phone found in the portable bass violin case at the Met during their investigation of Enrico's murder.

There it was, direct contact by the Prince with the murderer.

Damning evidence number two, almost enough to indict.

CHAPTER 34

It took two days and four gelatos (stracciatella, chocolato, mantucca and something described as "tabasco/kale-like") until the files were finally received. Another day was required to pore over them and assign follow-up responsibilities to the squad members.

The responsibility of directly confronting the Prince was again left to Laticco and Franco.

Extradition of a Prince.

Not exactly the easiest task that Laticco or even the Italian Government had ever faced.

"Not an easy task" was not an understatement. It had to first be approved and signed by the Prime Minister, followed by a confidential vote of the Senate security committee. Not everyone would be on board until they were privy to the overwhelming evidence and the absolute need for international closure.

Two telephone calls determined that the Prince was currently at his home at Lake Como near the top of the Italian "Boot." A third call commandeered a police jet to get the team there by early afternoon. The fourth call organized local police transportation and assistance, as might be needed.

In all his years on the NY Police Force, Franco had never seen such seamless and instantaneous organization.

Needless to say, but I will anyway, he was impressed.

A black Fiat van, complete with a GPS, local maps and local police backup awaited them at the Como airport. The Prince's manor house was highlighted on the map in royal red.

The fifteen-minute drive from the airport took them along the Western shore of the grand lake, past the famed Villa d'Este Hotel to his sumptuous 150-acre estate on the Lake Como shoreline.

Not exactly a shabby address.

The fleet of six black vans and an ambulance pulled up to the estate gatehouse at four that afternoon. The cavalcade included Laticco in the lead, eight police officers, a physician, two nurses, four aides and Franco. Their seven blaring sirens could be heard halfway round the world.

They showed their credentials to the security guard at the front gate and were given driving instructions on how to get the main house.

Yes, it was that big an estate.

Another seven-minute drive along curved roads brought them to the front entrance of a not-so-shabby three-story palazzo where they were met by the butler and another security officer.

Four of the officers were posted to cover the outside of the building should an escape be attempted.

After yet another check of their credentials they were escorted up the stairs, through the front hall and into the reception parlor.

Franco was out of breath, not as a result of the long walk, but because of the dazzling beauty of his immediate surroundings, especially the furniture, paintings, murals and grand ceilings. It wasn't often that he got to see Da Vinci's "Madonna of the Rocks," Titian's "Assumption of the Virgin," Rubens's "Rape of the Sabines," and Michelangelo's original maquette of the "David" in such an intimate setting. Franco could not begin to fathom that this was only part of the collection of just one person and it was, of course, echoed by other majestic works in his other mansions.

They were ushered to a seating area where they were told to make themselves comfortable. The Prince's emissary would be down in a few minutes.

This was the first time that Franco's tush had actually felt the cushion of a 17th century chair.

Franco's reverie was interrupted by the arrival of a 6'2" tall, rather

Murder at the Met

thin, pale-faced elderly gentleman with pince-nez glasses perched on the edge of his generous nose. He had seen pictures of historic figures like Teddy Roosevelt with these silly looking eyeglasses, but had never actually seen them in or on the flesh. The gentleman was immaculately dressed in razor sharp pleated trousers, tailed morning coat and of course a black bow tie. It was like walking back into history, especially within the setting he found himself.

This was not the Prince but the major domo, chief of household staff.

Laticco announced, "We have a warrant for the arrest of Prince Emanuel and are to be shown to his room immediately."

The butler protested and said that the Prince was seriously ill and under doctor's orders not to be disturbed.

"No one enters his room without the doctor's permission, not even me."

Laticco glared at him and barked, "You lead us to his room and unlock the door at once or I will have you arrested for obstruction of justice. Do you understand?"

"Sir, I completely understand but I can do nothing as I do not even have a key to his room. I have not even seen the interior of his chambers in close to four months. Only his doctor, his nurse and his private secretary possess such a key. They arrange for his health care, nutrition, medication, special equipment and other needs. I see to the functioning of the rest of the estate.

His personal team are all in his chambers as we speak."

Laticco got directions to the private chambers (a GPS would have been helpful), brushed past the butler and led his team up the wide staircase to the second level. He stationed one of the officers at the top and turned left with the rest of the team.

The massive hand-carved oak door directly ahead was his destination.

He knocked quite loudly while shouting, "This is the Federal Police, open this door immediately."

There was no response.

He repeated his demand, gave it a few moments and when there was no answer, he ordered the battering ram to be used.

One percussive swipe was enough to elicit, "Wait a second, I am trying to unlock it."

After a few seconds, there was a loud click and the door swung wide open. Three people stood facing the team, blocking the entrance of Laticco and his team to the room.

The short pudgy man with horn rimmed glasses in the middle said, "I am Doctor Mesta, the Prince's private physician, and I will not allow you to see him at this time because of his extremely delicate health. An alarming situation could prove to be fatal."

The tall, good-looking man in an expensive-looking black suit held up his hand in the pose of a traffic warden and said, "As the Prince's private secretary, I order you to leave at once."

Laticco pushed his way into the room and said, "You must either be hard of hearing or quite stupid. I don't believe that either one is the case.

I hold in my hand a warrant for the arrest of the Prince, now. It is personally signed by the Foreign Minister of the Government of Italy and is to be actioned on this date, and that is exactly why we are here. Is there anything of what I have just said that you do not understand?"

Laticco pushed right through the three men who reluctantly gave way. That was a good move on their part as Laticco was looking for an excuse to cuff them and haul their asses away.

Leaving one officer to guard the door to the hallway, with orders that no one was to enter or leave. Laticco, Franco and the rest of the group made their way across the antechamber to the only other door, obviously the entry to the bedroom.

This one was unlocked.

Laticco pushed it open. The room was pitch black dark with a faintly detectable perfume-like smell in the air and a whirring sound. He reached to his right and found the light switch on the wall.

The room was suddenly washed with a glaring light. The unfolding scene looked like it had escaped from a science fiction movie. A cheaply-made one, at that.

A single bed was in the center of the room, completely encapsulated by a giant clear plastic wall with tubes and wiring running to it. What was even stranger were the contents of the capsule lying on top of the bed. It was a human form! More importantly, it resembled the Prince. Even more importantly, it did not appear to be moving.

Doctor Mesta immediately tried to block their view and said, "The

Prince is in a coma within the hyperbaric chamber and cannot be disturbed. You must leave immediately."

While he was making this emphatic statement, the police doctor was peering at various charts, tanks and the patient.

"This man is not in a coma. He is dead.

The tanks are pumping nitrogen, not oxygen, into the chamber. His coloration suggests that he has been dead for some extended period of time and the nitrogen is delaying his body's decomposition, possibly to minimize attendant odors and/or mask the actual time of his demise. Without a proper autopsy, we cannot rule out the possibility of foul play. This could very well be a murder scene."

Laticco immediately gave instructions to his group. "Officers place these three gentlemen in custody, and bring them downtown. The initial charges are for interfering with the cause of justice and illegally harboring a deceased person. We will expand the charges as we learn more about the conditions surrounding the Prince's death. Secure the premises as a crime scene and hold all resident staff in custody as potential witnesses. No one is permitted to enter without my personal clearance.

Further, all staff will be held incommunicado and to be released only on my direct orders.

Doctor Mesta, please arrange to have the deceased immediately transported to the Medical Examiner's office."

The organization, speed and absolute efficiency of the operation under the direction of Chief Detective Laticco was once again an absolute eye opener even for the well experienced Franco.

No red tape, no bureaucratic interference, just one seamless and professional operation.

CHAPTER 35

Laticco opened the early morning team meeting with, "Doctor Mesta's autopsy report does not indicate any evidence of foul play. The prince apparently died of natural causes, but here is the kicker, that was at least four months ago. The three musketeers who were incarcerated last week are no longer considered to be murder suspects. After consultation with the Federal Attorney's office, it was advised that they should be immediately released, but under certain conditional restraints, as they still stand accused of interfering with a police investigation and illegally harboring a corpse.

The reasons behind their strange behavior are still under investigation. Therefore their travels from their respective homes will be limited to a one-mile radius, to be tracked by ankle bracelets. Their passports are to be impounded and the ability to communicate with each other must be absolutely blocked.

Questions?"

"Yes, Chief," said one of the officers. "Where does our investigation go from here? What are our assignments?"

"You are always one step ahead of me, Arturo, and that is to be commended. I was about to address those specific points.

There are a number of questions that must be answered during the course of this ongoing investigation. These are only the ones that I am currently familiar with. As we make progress, additional areas will undoubtedly surface.

Let us consider the following:

Why was the prince's death being held secret?
Why was his body hidden from even his household staff?
What was to be gained or lost by the above actions?
What is the full extent of others who may be involved?
How does the above tie in with the events in the US, which is the reason for Franco joining us in Italy?

When we have answers to these questions, the investigation will tell us where to go from there."

Laticco then proceeded to hand out assignments to each of his officers.

What he thought would prove to be the key to the whole affair was assigned to his financial forensics specialist. That involved the detailed analysis of the prince's vast holdings.

"I want you to go over all of his personal and corporate papers, ledgers and accounts. Wills are of special interest and to be given to me, as I will personally follow that trail. As we all know, the prince never married and is not known to have any direct or (ahem) indirect heirs. As you may recall, the forensic report, coupled with his personal physician's notes, indicate that the prince's sperm count was much too low to impregnate any potential child carrier.

"Where does his vast fortune go?"

A few telephone calls were placed and by freely using the Minister's name, appointments were made.

"Franco, grab your coat, we are off to pay a visit to the prince's personal attorney, the renowned Sergio Baldesteri, lawyer to the really BIG names. Not big, as in height, but BIG as in personal wealth and influence. He is the one who recently got former Prime Minister Berlusconi released from all charges. It cost his client a small fortune, but he saved the former Prime Minister's personal humongous holdings, and incidentally, saved his client from incarceration."

The Fiat and driver (also part of Laticco's team) were waiting in the parking area adjacent to the Ministry. Laticco gave the driver directions to the Attorney's office. Said directions were not really necessary as Sgnr.

Baldesteri's address was well known to all Romans. Although unknown to the general public, his office was situated at the top level of the Coliseum.

Yes, the Coliseum.

The real one.

Just being rich was not enough to get the permits needed for this very special location. One had to be rich and have essentially every politician in his pocket. Baldesteri had in his 30-year career saved essentially every major politico's ass.

He had acquired this prime space and managed to install hidden plumbing, power, phone, fax, heat, air conditioning, one-way windows and even an elevator, without general public awareness.

You remember the pictures of the costumed Praetorian guards who stand outside the wall to pose for pictures with tourists (and Franco), who pay for the photo privilege. Their real prime function is that of outer perimeter security guards for Baldesteri. They form the first line of defense against angry clients and/or public reaction to those same clients. No, he does not keep lions in the arena pit as a second line of defense! But under any circumstances do not get the elevator operator pissed off.

Their car parked in the reserved space that was under the control of the guards. One flash of Laticco's credentials kept the guards at bay and allowed them to go back to their other work for tips.

Laticco and Franco followed the guard's directions and walked through the maze of tunnels behind the outer wall, crossed some roped-off areas, and found the elevator behind a closed, battered wooden door with an old iron knocker. The door was reinforced by a full-length hidden slab of two-inch-thick steel. If you didn't know it was there, you were not meant to know that it was there.

Laticco knocked three times to summon the elevator operator. You have this image of the warriors who were thrown into the arena to battle each other, and/or the lion? The guy who answered the knock was twice as big and much uglier. It was Brutus, or someone who resembled our image of him, who re-checked their credentials.

Even Laticco called him sir!

Notification by the guards outside was enough for Brutus to carry them to the top floor. The only other elevator stop, which was now by-passed, was on the floor below, where the other guards had their lounge and equipment.

They entered a stark modern reception area decorated with black and white furniture, matching furnishings and two beautiful blond secretary types. They both had Glock pistols in their waistbands. These ladies were obviously not just there for decoration.

After a second check of their ID's and permits to carry firearms, they were escorted into the inner sanctum.

What they saw was mind-blowing.

The room was huge with plush red carpeting, black and white furniture and DaVinci Resurrection paintings hung on each of the two side walls.

Yes, real ones.

The outside wall, which was nothing more than a huge one-way window had a view of the arena three stories below. One could almost hear the clash of swords, the roar of the lion and the chanting of the crowd. For some reason the smell of hotdogs and beer was not present.

His desk and chair were mounted on a turntable so that he could work when alone with the view of the arena directly in front of him. When there were visitors, as was now the case, the desk and chairs were soundlessly electrically rotated to face the center of the room.

"Good morning, gentlemen. I assume that this is not just a casual visit. How can I help you?"

Laticco said, "I have been appointed by the Foreign Minister to look into the affairs of Prince Emanuel on an extremely confidential basis regarding a matter that is currently privy only to the Minister and my team. This is Detective Franco, an American, who has been assigned as a liaison case officer in this investigation."

After declining the hospitable offer of a traditional morning Grappa, coffees and biscotti were brought in while Baldesteri was read the official secrets act. He was then sworn to absolute confidentiality. It was then, and only then, that Laticco was able to recount the background to this investigation and what was needed from him.

"I understand where you are coming from and, as an ethical attorney, financial advisor and Italian citizen, I will cooperate to my fullest extent. It is my absolute hope that this investigation will ultimately lead to the innocence and vindication of my dear departed friend, Prince Emanuel.

I was told by my secretary that you would require certain information.

Some of the records you seek are right here and can be available by this afternoon, but others are located at various offices, banks and homes around the country. It will take some time to collect copies, especially since most of this has to be done surreptitiously. I will get the process started as soon as you leave, but how else can I help you right now?"

Laticco thanked him and said, "I will have one of my team here later in the day to pick up what you have assembled. He will use the code word "Enrico" to identify himself. Because of the sensitivity of this investigation, this code word will be used by members of our team throughout the investigation. Should it be compromised, I will personally so inform you.

On behalf of the Minister and myself, we thank you for your understanding and cooperation."

They left via the same route as their entry, thus judiciously avoided ending up in the arena where there were still visions of hungry lions and warriors.

Even hefty armed policemen can have daytime nightmares.

"That went better than I had expected," Laticco mused.

CHAPTER 36

By the time they got back to Laticco's office, an autopsy report was sitting on his desk. It confirmed that the Prince's death was of natural causes, most likely a stroke. They were still running toxicology tests, but were reasonably sure that they would prove to be negative. The medical examiner also confirmed that death had occurred at least three, probably four, months ago.

"So," Laticco said to the assembled team, "this tells us that the Prince was not directly involved at the time of Enrico's death in the US. However, it does not tell us if he had at some point given instructions to do the dirty deed.

Our investigation now lies in the detailed examination of his private papers as well as his financial and other documentation. You all have your assignments.

Tonight does not exist! We will all be here 26 hours a day until we have screened every scrap of paper, every computer file and have prepared our verbal summaries. We need proof of his role in the murder. Meals will be provided; however, you will be limited to one glass each of Chianti per meal (except with your breakfast cappuccino) so that you will remain coherent.

Questions?"

No questions. These seasoned detectives knew exactly what to do and returned to their respective work stations to begin the process of wearing out their eyes and numbing their brains.

By dinner time the next day the team re-assembled to deliver their findings. Franco was absolutely transfixed at how every member showed no visible sign of their two-day non-sleep marathon, and unlike his own experience at the Precinct back home, no one bitched, not even in jest.

After about three hours of presentations of findings, some sense of direction was beginning to form.

The investigators had not only found written confirmation of the Prince's orders to his Foundation in New York about payment for the prescription sedative, but equally important, instructions as to who was to pick it up, one Dr. Stinton.

There it was, the primary hard evidence needed to link the Prince to the murder. There was only one teeny-weeny little problem.

It was written about two months after the Prince had died.

Further digging into travel logs and credit card expenditures revealed that the orders had been written in the Prince's palazzo in Rome on the very day that his financial advisor and personal assistant were there. Essentially, all of the rest of the time they spent in Lake Como isolating the Prince's body from all but the three who were aware of his demise.

A further in-depth search revealed the original will of King Emanuel I. It left his total estate to be equally apportioned only to his direct living heirs, to be done this very year. Along with the will was a second very secret parchment detailing his liaison with a certain courtesan, Contessa Cornelia, and her eventual birth of a boy child, which the King acknowledged to be his own son.

The parchment further detailed how this illegitimate, but acknowledged son and his other direct heirs were to be protected through the generations. Reference was made to certain secret friends and "family" members who were entrusted with this on-going task. They were all named in this document.

There was a "family" name specified and tasked with having absolute responsibility through the generations to ensure that his will, and its direct heirs, be covertly taken under their wings.

This blood vow to the King taken by the then Don Corezzo was held to be sacred through the ages until the present day, where it was still absolutely enforced by the current Don Corezzo, still acknowledged as "Boss of Bosses."

"OK, Franco, pack your bags. You and I are about to take a little trip to the really small town of Corezzo, in Sicily." Laticco then made some discreet phone calls to associates in Palermo, the capital of Sicily.

By nightfall, the ministry plane carrying Laticco and Franco touched down at the Palermo airport, and they were met by a black Mercedes SUV. The sole occupant was Chief Superintendent Gaspari, the highest ranking police officer in Sicily. He was entrusted with the mission of their trip. This was absolutely necessary, as Gaspari was to be the go-between in setting up a secret meeting with Don Corezzo.

In Sicily, nothing is as it seems. You might even recall when former President Kennedy called upon "Lucky" Luciano, the American Mafia Don, who after his exile from the USA, became "Boss-of-Bosses" in Sicily, to help with the assassination of President Castro during the Cuban missile crisis. It never actually came about, but the "door" was open to discussion.

The enemy is at times your friend and your friend is sometimes your brother-in-law. A true symbiotic relationship, with a convenient on/off switch.

Indeed, Gaspari was married to the daughter of Don Corezzo. This was not such an unusual relationship for a relatively small island. It was well known to all and did not taint the integrity of either party's responsibilities. It did, however, open the door for Laticco and Franco to have a face-to-face meeting with the Don.

The drive from the airport to the surrounding countryside passed through an invisible line that might just as well have been a steel barrier. The city side was an unending, sometimes crumbling mixture of churches, small shops, cliff dweller mass housing and two-room ancient houses all linked by pot-holed streets.

The other side was verdant, fresh and clear farmland.

They passed by beautiful vineyards with the aroma of ripening grapes and an almost endless line of various fruit orchards with the justly famed calamari tomato farms sprinkled in between.

Palermo was Sicily's Detroit and Santa Barbara, rolled into one.

After a wonderful one-hour drive, they approached the town of Corezzo.

The town became increasingly more attractive as they approached the center. It began to look much like a coffee table picture book's photos of beautiful ancient landmarks. Franco was so entranced that he was hardly aware of Gaspari's briefing. Laticco's elbow in Franco's ribs brought him back to the moment.

"Let me do the talking. The Don and I are old friends and he does not make new ones easily. As a matter of fact, if you say the wrong thing it could put you in harm's way. Even my esteemed colleague from Rome would not be protected by his badge. This is a harsh thing for me to say, especially knowing my position in protecting the public. However, a fact of life is still a fact of life. So, until I signal that you may speak, keep your lips stitched together.

Capeesh?"

"Yes, Chief Superintendent," was Laticco's simple response.

The car pulled onto one of the rare inner-town tree-lined streets with lovely homes on either side of the road. "Needless to say, but I will anyway," as they drove through steel gates, "this is the largest home in the area. Quite possibly the largest in the province.

Not quite possibly, it really is the largest."

As police professionals, they silently acknowledged the number of security cameras mounted all along the driveway from the entry to the front door. They had been ID'ed and granted admission without a spoken word.

The Don, himself, opened the door, embraced his son-in-law and ushered them into his "modest" little home. Franco's practiced eye, after all he had been looking to move to a house in the New York suburbs for the last two years, estimated, based on this urban lot size, the external house footprint and the size of the reception area, that "modest" meant at least 20,000 sq. ft. Franco often went to a local movie emporium in Flatbush that was half the size of this house. His own current apartment could easily fit into just the entry area.

After introductions, the Don led them down a short corridor, through very thick and elegantly carved ancient oak doors into his study. The room was not much smaller than the reception area, but much more elaborately decorated. At Franco's silent guesstimate of 2,000 sq. ft., it was not quite large enough to be used as a basketball court. However, it was of sufficient size to accommodate the sensational collection of art and furniture it held. The paintings were all so familiar, mostly Italian classic artists including the requisite DaVinci and Michelangelo. There were also two contemporary paintings that beautifully complemented the older ones. Franco did not even have to guess that they were Barbara Gray's. They just seemed to turn up everywhere.

The Don ignored his desk and the two chairs in front of it in favor of the delicately carved settee with red silk cushions, four renaissance gilt chairs and an elaborate eighteenth century coffee table. Three cups of espresso, a crystal decanter of Grappa and three Murano glasses graced the table.

Now that I think of it, "graced" may be the wrong adjective to describe the Grappa. If you've ever drunk the stuff you would know that "scarred" would be a more appropriate description.

To paraphrase Mel Brooks in his early film, *A History of The World, Part I*, "It's good to be the Don."

After seating his guests and presenting the libation, the Don asked, "Now, my dear son-in-law and his esteemed colleagues, what can I do for you?"

As agreed beforehand, Gasparri took the lead. He gave an elaborate introduction of Laticco and Franco, their titles, the close relationship between the Italian and American governments and the absolute personal backing of the Italian president on this very sensitive matter.

He continued with a complete briefing, starting with the murder of Enrico in New York, and the investigation to date, all leading to the Prince's direct involvement.

"Now, dear Don, we desperately need your help to see that the American son of a hard-working Italian immigrant to the United States is recognized as the great-great grandson and direct heir of King Emanuel I. When that has been accomplished, the case against the people responsible for that murder and the attempt to steal the fortune from a fine Italian family will fall in line.

We seek justice in the broadest sense of the word. It is a justice that involves family wishes and honor! That is something that all in this room can relate to."

The Don was silent, thinking for a few moments about what he had just learned, and then he said, "I hear you and must say that I agree with your motivation in this case. No one knows better than I and understands the importance of absolutely heeding the wishes of one's family. Family is the core of one's being. Family is the spine of each one of us. Without family, we wander alone and are defenseless in the wilderness.

It is my absolute desire to help you. Tell me what it is you need from me."

"My esteemed father-in-law," replied Gaspari, "thank you for your wise words. I am but recently introduced to the problem we face, so let me have my colleagues address the specifics. First Francesco Di Angelo, an American Detective with the New York City Police Department. He has been involved with the investigation into the murder of an innocent young second-generation Italian-American named Enrico Calzoni.

Francesco, could you brief the Don on the background and current status of your investigation?"

Franco spent the next hour relating to the Don the peculiar circumstances of the murder, the background of the deceased, the implications of his family history and finally, the evident link to the prince that they had found.

The Don questioned him extensively about what they had determined about Enrico's grandfather and his relationship with the then current Don of Corezzo del Marno. He also asked for more detailed information about what they knew about that Don's summons to visit King Victor Emanuel I.

It was apparent from his line of questioning that the royal visit made by Don Corezzo so many years ago was not exactly news to this present day Don of Dons.

After Don Corezzo was satisfied that he had enough background from Franco, the story was continued by Detective Laticco.

Laticco related the course of their investigation in Italy, which even further complicated the Prince's involvement. Laticco ended his input with their surprise finding that the Prince was dead and this had been hidden from all but three individuals for the last three months.

Clearly one or all of the three who were aware of the Prince's demise were involved in the murder of Enrico. This was obvious as Enrico was murdered about two months <u>after</u> the Prince had died. The big question was, did they act on their own or was it under specific instructions from the Prince? If instructed to do so, how did they benefit?

Again, the Don sat silently, with eyes closed, for a few minutes while absorbing the myriad of facts that had been unearthed to date and presented to him. He puffed on his morning cigar, had a sip of grappa, opened his eyes and in his gravelly voice said, "You must understand, I normally would not make the following statement to the police, but my lifelong friendship with, and allegiance to the Prince, trumps all of my usual feelings.

What is it I can do to help your investigation?"

Laticco responded, "There is a critical piece of the puzzle that is still missing. We don't have the original will. We need to confirm that the original document signed by King Victor Emanuel 1 outlining the distribution of his estate after his demise is still in existence, and equally important, we need to know who were designated as the beneficiaries."

"I know of what you speak," said the Don. "The parchment you seek has been entrusted to my possession and to those of my forbears for three generations. Had I known of the Prince's demise, I would have followed the accompanying instructions and immediately turned it over to his lawyers and made it public. Those were his expressed wishes!

It is because I am part of a very special "family" that I will only release these papers and accompanying instructions to you on a very confidential basis. No one may be made privy to where these papers came from. I mean no one!

However, should word of my action become public knowledge, be prepared to continuously look behind you for the rest of your certain-to-be-shortened life.

Understand?"

He then walked over to the wall to the right of the settee and gently slid the painting of *The School of Athens*, by Michelangelo on hidden rails, to the right. Behind the crowd in the painting was a hinged steel plate about three feet square. A push button combination lock and eye scanner were then used to gain entry.

The massive door smoothly and noiselessly slid open.

The Don put on cotton gloves that had been stored just in back of the door of the safe. He reached in and pulled out a ribbon-bound scrolled parchment from the bottom shelf. The safe was then closed and Mike's masterpiece was returned to its original position.

He gently placed the parchment on the table, removed the ribbon and unfurled Emanuel's will. It certainly looked bona fide, royal seal, illumination, et al.

Laticco then spent the next hour trying to understand and finally orally translate it. He was reasonably accurate, considering that the old Roman dialect was written in cursive script.

There were no surprises.

It was exactly as Elaine's lawyer, Mr. Welling, had described it, but at last they actually had the physical evidence in hand. No surprises! The entire estate was to remain intact until the eightieth anniversary of Immanuel's death. It was then to be equally distributed only to his living direct heirs. There was even the specific mention of his illegitimate son as a true heir.

As important as this parchment was, it was but one of the missing pieces needed to prove Enrico Calzoni's true and legal lineage back to the throne.

This one-page parchment had a current estimated value of some five billion dollars. To put that in perspective, it took J.K. Rowling many thousands of pages to earn just one-fifth of that amount, and she is the second richest woman in Great Britain. Care to guess who is the richest?

Hint: Her title is Queen.

"I believe that I can further assist the offspring of the late Mr. Calzoni," interjected the Don. "I have been entrusted with another set of documents by my forbears with instructions to release them to the appropriate authorities at the appropriate time. It would appear that this is the appropriate time and of course the appropriate authorities would be you, my dear son-in-law."

He once again opened the wall safe and removed another scrolled parchment. When unfurled and stretched out, it was about two feet square. A quick glance showed it to be a family genealogy chart with King Emanuel 1 at the top.

It clearly showed two distinct and equally weighted lines of descent. One line led from Emanuel and his queen through the generations to the current Prince. Each generation added after Emanuel's death was appropriately witnessed by court notaries and the then current Dons. The current Don had added a witnessed notation some years earlier that the current Prince was the last in his line as he was not married and routine medical tests had shown him to be impotent.

There was also the parallel line of descent from Emanuel and his courtesan, Contessa Cornelia. This, too, was attested to by the same officials and the then current Dons. It ended with Enrico Calzoni. His death was verified in the document by the current Don and the managing attorney from Welling's Rome office.

At last it became apparent how Welling knew of Calzoni's involvement in Emanuel's estate.

What the Don was totally unaware of was the continuation of Enrico Calzoni's direct lineage in the fetus now being carried by Enrico's fiancée. With the written attestation of all present in the room, the Don added "Bambino Calzoni, to be verified by DNA tests," to the document.

Copies were immediately made of both documents and presented to each in the room. The originals were presented to Lattico for further safekeeping as evidence to be used in the courts of law of several countries.

Said evidence would serve a triple purpose in the courts. Firstly, the proof of rightful lineage in dividing the estate. Secondly, it would serve as evidence in the murder trial of Enrico Calzoni's killer in the US. Finally, it would be used as evidence in Italy as to the complicity of the Prince's three confidants in the act of premeditated murder.

A smiling Franco had to then describe his statement about their hitting a "A three Bagger."

"My dear son-in-law and new friend, you would do me much honor if you would join me in a humble lunch before continuing on your important journey."

After much insistence, and feigned resistance, they finally accepted the Don's kind offer of a simple lunch before they left. For Franco, it would have been one of life's biggest boo-boos not to have accepted.

Lunch was as delicious to him as a wet dream would be for a man on a deserted island. Everything he had at home, multiplied by a factor of ten on the scrumptious scale, was serially served starting at one pm. For the next three hours of pure bliss, Franco had such treats as Caprese salad made with firm tomatoes grown on the farms they had just passed, topped with that morning's freshly made mozzarella from the Don's goats' milk, extra-extra-extra-extra virgin olive oil from the Don's olive grove and fresh basil from the Don's adjacent farm.

That was just the opener!

Each succeeding course, with appropriate wines, was the "nth" degree in taste of anything he had ever had before. The pasta course was a fettuccine Alfredo following a recipe handed down to the Don's father by Chef Alfredo a half a century ago. Pure bliss! From the estate's vineyard on the mainland, a Montepulciano d'Abruzzo, which seemed like it had been aged and bottled just for this course, on this particular day, for consumption at 2:00 in the afternoon.

The fish course was a simple, but exquisite Dover sole, caught only that morning and flown in from London. It had an almond butter preparation that floated into one's mouth. The accompanying Santa Margarita Pinot Grigio was not exactly schlocky.

Finally, as if the Don somehow knew of Franco's secret weakness (maybe his widespread "family" did know), when dessert arrived, it was a homemade stracciatella gelato.

It tasted like the Italian gods had only reluctantly provided the Don's chef with the recipe because they knew that Franco would be at his table.

Even the after-dinner Grappa smoothly flowed down his gullet without making a coarse file out of his throat!

After many *grazies* and *buongiornos*, they took their very satisfied leave and headed directly to the airport for the flight back to Rome.

Oh! the wonderful and fulfilling dreams that invaded Franco's nap during the one-hour flight.

He could not fully understand any of them as they were all in Italian.

However, the dreams still tasted great.

CHAPTER 37

"Franco, you put on weight," was the universal greeting that the usually only modestly overweight Franco heard upon his return to the Precinct.

However, the kidding tone was well tempered by the congratulations he received from all on the success of his trip. The certified copies of the papers he brought back would serve as the backbone of the continuing murder investigation in the US.

Connie now had the evidence to charge the murderer, but first one little detail, they had to find him.

Little details.

They were holed up in a corner of the squad room so that Franco could give Connie his full oral report. (He judiciously left out details of the number of gelatos consumed.) In return, Connie filled him in on progress made at home.

"While you were expanding your girth with all sorts of delectable goodies, we have not exactly been sitting on our hands. First, I want Ozzie to brief you on his findings in Indianapolis.

Hey Ozzie, do you have a few minutes?"

There is only one acceptable answer to a question like that from the boss.

"Yes, sir, be right in.

Welcome back, mate. Franco, it looks like you put on a few kilos."

With Connie's well-known, universal look, Ozzie knew it was his cue to stop the kidding and start the fill-in.

"My few days in Indianapolis uncovered a treasure trove of background information that put the murder in historical perspective. With the help of the locals and the newspaper's morgue, we were able to trace the victim's family history.

We now have a paper trail that begins with his father, Pietro Calzoni, moving from New York City within days of his ship's landing in 1925. There was no record of any contacts he may have made prior to the train ride to Indianapolis or why he picked that particular location to finally settle in. However, within ten years of the move, there were Indianapolis City Hall records that approved his opening a men's apparel shop in the downtown area.

The first big question was how could this penniless immigrant save enough to invest in such a costly enterprise? A little more digging uncovered a financial backer, a Mr. Giorgio Lamandi.

It did not take much effort to uncover Mr. Lamandi's interest in the business, or in anything else on the shadier side of the street. He was well known to the authorities and the general public as the "Boss" in the greater Indianapolis area.

Now comes the really strange part. There was absolutely no record of any intervention by Mr. Lamandi or associates in the store, even as it grew through so many years.

No debt payments.

No torchings.

No stolen merchandise.

Nada.

He was not just a silent investor, it was as if he was never involved.

From clippings, it was apparent that the growth of this small shop was a result of management by one who was a natural retailer. He not only knew his clientele, but also nurtured his small staff and selected the right suppliers. He instinctively did everything right and the enterprise continued to grow.

The only other time that Mr. Lamandi's name appeared in connection to the store was in 1954, when a huge project was undertaken to build a one-square-block emporium that is still the retail centerpiece of the downtown area.

Between City Hall records and newspaper morgue clippings, we were able to uncover the intervention of one Mr. Lamandi in expediting city certifications and settling construction labor and supplier problems.

Once the new Emporium opened, the name Lamandi never came up again.

During the early days of the first shop, Pietro fell in love with a lovely Italian immigrant introduced to him by a friend in the Italian Social Club. They married after a one-year courtship and soon, but not too soon, produced a boy child they named Enrico. Unfortunately, Enrico never knew his mother as she died in childbirth.

The rest of the story was one that we are all are familiar with. Enrico exhibited a huge musical talent from the age of six, when he started to play the piano. Not just bang on the keys or play "Chopsticks." He imitated études he had heard just once on dad's radio! He even played variations on them. This was a force that had to be further developed, and his dad made it a major focus.

He ultimately won entrance to the Juilliard School of Music where he spent four years honing his prodigious skill. After graduation, Enrico was brought on board by the respected Classical Artists Talent Agency in New York before his move back to Indianapolis to live with his ailing dad.

Although dad's heart condition was not then life threatening, Enrico thought it prudent to spend whatever time he had between recitals throughout the States with him. Apparently father and son had that close a relationship.

Then in June of 2006, the inevitable.

Pietro's life and Enrico's musical career ended in one last heartbeat.

The entire city of Indianapolis mourned the passing of this well-beloved immigrant citizen who had lived the American dream in a manner that respected and helped all that he had come in contact with. Via his extensive charitable work, his reach extended to a vast number of people he had never met.

As an only child, Enrico was suddenly thrust into the running of the family business, thus ending his musical journey.

All of his energy and innate business talent was expended in the continuation of his father's work, both in the business as well as in good deeds. The enterprise continued to prosper. His long hours of involvement left little, if any, time to maintain his first love, the piano.

That is, until he got that life changing call from Juilliard to visit Kokomo. It was then that Enrico found his new first love, Elaine. All else in his life fell into a distant second place.

During his first year of courting young Elaine to be his life partner, he started to solidify his own plan of how to live that conjoined life. Enrico spent many restless days and nights perfecting the scenario for the rest of their days.

We all are familiar with the rest of the story, the sale of the business, the move to New York and the plans for marriage as well as the plans for a parallel return to the performance arena along with his wife-to-be.

The one major thing I could not find after the sale of the business was some form of repayment to his dad's original investors. All of the purchase funds, with the exception of taxes paid, remained the sole possession of Enrico, to be later passed on to his fiancée as per his latest will.

A check with his attorney and the various tax authorities validated all of the above.

It was all perfectly kosher.

CHAPTER 38

A quick headcount showed all to be present.

Connie waited for the morning ritual of distribution of macchiatos, lattes, americanos, etc., finding their ultimate consumers. Whatever happened to the good old tasteless and gritty coffee-like liquid that flavored, pumped and destroyed our veins in years gone by?

But I digress.

"Alright people, we have work to do. You have all read the reports to date and know the background. Our Italian colleagues are pursuing the money trail behind the hiring of our assassin. They will deal with the three individuals apparently behind the scheme and at the same time see if they will be able to clear the Prince's name.

All we have to do is catch the son-of-a-bitch who did the dirty.

There has been a BOLO out on an international level with the perp's description, his known aliases and preferred modes of transportation. He has always been a loner, so there are no known contacts to keep eyes on. As far as we know he has not left the country, so it is still up to us.

You will work in pre-assigned teams. Your partners are already known to you and each team has received a packet that includes your specific assignment. You are all highly trained police officers and have well-earned promotions into this group. You are not robots, so use your intuition and follow leads wherever they go. If it wanders into someone else's area of responsibility, speak to that fellow lead officer and mutually determine who does what. Just follow the trail! Report back to me as anything significant arises.

That's it.

Questions?

None?

Dismissed."

Within fifteen minutes the squad room was abandoned by all but four detectives working the phones and/or checking papers. The room hummed with activity and a noise level as if all 20 officers were still there.

Franco joined Connie at his desk to discuss liaison with Rome and what other areas of investigation were not covered by the group that just left the building.

"Franco, I would like you to also remain in at least daily contact with Rome so that we are all up to date on mutual progress. It is obviously essential that anything solid that they may turn up involving communication with our suspect be made available to us. We have to get more information about his modus operandi after his past "projects" were completed. Where did he go? Abroad or domestic? Aliases? Contacts?

We need a more complete picture.

We need a starting point.

I know this may be hard, wink, wink, nod, nod, but I still want you to maintain daily contact with Ms Jones and her security team. Report back to me if anything smells un-kosher.

Go."

Franco returned to his desk and immediately placed his first call to Rome. The timing was perfect as it would be late afternoon in Rome and Laticco would likely still be at his desk.

"Si, Laticco, *buon pomeriggio*! Oh, it's you Franco. How was the trip home? Etc. etc."

After the requisite niceties, the conversation turned to the necessities.

Franco explained the reason for the call and established a timeframe for the future daily calls. He specifically noted to Laticco the need for something solid tying Rome to their suspect. If they should uncover anything further about how he was introduced, who the intermediary was, how communications to him were handled and how he was paid, the investigation would have a starting point.

Murder at the Met

"I am in complete agreement," Laticco interjected. "Obviously, we understand your needs and will try our best to see what we can uncover to help you.

Speak to you tomorrow."

Franco then placed the first of his daily calls and increasing trips to the Jones residence.

They were now on a first name basis.

At Connie's request, Franco joined him in going through the boxes of reports stacked next to his desk. Each box contained detailed information garnered by the various detectives during the course of the last three weeks since the murder. This was definitely not the glamorous side of the homicide detective's workday. Car chases, shoot-outs, forensic revelations as seen on TV, are rarely the essence of a homicide detective's work. The health downside of this basic office work were the constant coffee refills, necessitating a constant refill of the sweet and sticky "to-go-with" stuff.

Franco did not really need the latter as he was still recovering from gelato saturation (read: an additional two inches around the waist.)

After about an hour, Connie raised his hand and yelled across the desk to Franco, "Hey, I think I might have something here. This is the report submitted by Ozzie after his visit to Indianapolis last week. I remember reading it when it crossed my desk, but missed what could be a potential starting point. When coupled with information we have learned since his last visit, this has become more meaningful.

On page 2, last paragraph, it says, 'There were no other claims or liens on the property sold. It was free and clear with all of the proceeds going directly to Enrico Calzoni. The only outgoings were to pay federal, state and local taxes. Additionally, a week later, Calzoni made a payment of $2,000,000 to the loan agent of record, Mr. Salvatore Panzo.'

Franco, we initially just accepted this as a standard loan practice, but now it jumps out of the page and yells 'Whoa!'

Who is this Mr. Panzo? Is he a legitimate business broker? Is the amount appropriate for the total sale? Is this kosher?

My gut says let's dig.

I need to speak to Ozzie immediately and get his ass back to Indianapolis by tonight. I need to know more about this Mr. Salvatore Panzo.

Franco, get Ozzie moving yesterday."

CHAPTER 39

Ozzie checked in with his contacts from his visit just the week before, immediately after his plane touched down and the cab got him to Indianapolis Police Headquarters.

His quest was quite simple. Who was this Salvatore Panzo and what was known about him?

These questions had been raised the evening before, when he had called to make the appointment, so some answers were immediately available.

Apparently, Mr. Panzo was a well-known figure in the city as the number-two man in the local Social Club. The Club was well known for its charitable involvement with people in need, holiday gift distribution to children and its work resolving local disagreements. Additionally, they were also involved in: prostitution, protection, drug distribution, usury, gambling and other assistance to those in real need.

What a wonderful group of citizens.

The records filed with City Hall showed that when Mr. Calzoni built the present emporium, the largest single investor was the City Realty Development Group. It took the better part of the morning to comb through the interlocking nature of the principals of this organization. It distilled down to a core group consisting primarily of the CEO of the Social Club, one Mr. Salvatore Panzo.

There was no record of their involvement in the day-to-day operation of the Emporium. As a matter of fact, there was no record of their involvement until the payment by Mr. Calzoni to Mr. Panzo after the sale of the business. The most interesting thing about this repayment was that it was for the exact amount of the original loan, some 20 years earlier. There was no interest. No escalation in the principal amount for inflation.

Social Clubs are not usually known for their compassionate donations of business loans. Indeed, an investment of this type would have normally yielded at least a tenfold return. That, or bodies turning up in strange places. It was obvious from the papers that this was a final and equitable settlement between Mr. Calzoni and Mr. Panzo, with no bodies required.

Yet the subsequent finding of Mr. Calzoni's body a year later was very intriguing, and very real.

Further digging into the records showed that a check for twenty thousand dollars was sent from Panzo to Calzoni on the date of the announcement of Calzoni's engagement to Elaine. There was also a major party the next Saturday night in celebration of same. Enrico and Elaine flew back to Indianapolis for the weekend to accept all of the good wishes.

This was not exactly the prelude to a whack job.

The conclusion was that the Social Club was not responsible for said demise. There was a purely financial investment made at the beginning of the construction of the new store and said amount was returned in full at the sale of same. No record of further claims. No reports of animosity.

Everybody apparently happy.

Absolutely no linkage of the Indianapolis Social Club to Enrico's demise.

End of Social Club story.

CHAPTER 40

"The answers that we seek will be found in our own backyard with some important input from our Italian friends," Connie told the group assembled for their morning briefing. "Ozzie's findings indicate that further exploration in Indiana would not likely contribute anything more of use to our investigation. So, continue with your current assignments.

Ozzie, see me after we finish the group briefing for re-assignment."

After individual reports by the detectives and discussion of general housekeeping information, the group was dismissed.

"Ozzie, I would like you to team with Watkins and follow up with all of the federal agencies to see what they may have on our perp, and most importantly, if there is any suspected movement of his known aliases that may pop up from the various transportation groups. Obviously contact must be made not only with public and private airport authorities, but also with international shipping ports and border crossings. Also, about that last item, contact Canadian and Mexican authorities to see if their records show any anomalies.

Go."

The end of the discussion was the cue for Franco to now join Connie.

Connie was silent for the next few minutes, trying to work out an investigative starting point for Franco and himself. After nine years of having his professional skills molded by his close association with Connie,

Franco's mind was on exactly the same track. After some fifteen minutes, they both came to the same conclusion.

Nada.

The wheels spun for another twenty minutes when the first "Aha" was uttered by Connie.

"Obviously, we have to find the creep before he does any more damage. Why don't we start with Homeland Security? An individual with the record of international assassinations that our perp has must have left some tracks with that group. The Director of Special Operations, Michael McManus, was a former NYPD officer, who at one point partnered with my dad. The last time I saw him was probably at least twenty odd years ago when dad brought him home for dinner after a particularly grueling twenty-six hour hostage negotiation situation was successfully resolved.

I'll give him a buzz and remind him of the snotty little kid with a thousand questions who has yet one more."

The interdepartmental telephone contact directory located Director McManus's office in the Federal Building in downtown Manhattan. All interdepartmental telephone lines were secure and theoretically insulated from prying ears. Dialing only six digits from any phone in the system was required in order to directly contact anyone on the list. Connie had such a phone.

"Director McManus, this is Detective Lieutenant Connie Collins of the NYPD. I doubt that you would remember me from some twenty or so years ago, when you were a dinner guest at my dad's table and a bratty kid kept peppering you with inane questions about . . ."

"Connie, stop there," McManus interrupted. "Of course I remember you, and most certainly your late, great dad. He was a man's man, who earned every accolade and honor presented to him. He was a man who I learned so much from.

Why has it taken over twenty years to hear from you, and when can we get together? I need to catch up on your life beyond what I have read about in the papers every time you've solved a particularly perplexing case.

The Collins name still plays an important role in my continuing education."

"Well sir, beyond just wanting to re-establish an important childhood relationship with one of my personal heroes, I do need to pick your brain on a delicate case that I am now faced with. Toward that end, I wonder if your busy schedule has an hour or so when I could drop by your office?"

McManus countered with, "The father of modern psychology, Dr. Abraham Maslow, created his famed treatise "Hierarchy of Needs" in 1950. As this numb mind recalls, air is number one on the list followed by food, water, sex and so on. Until global warming reaches its full effect, air and water will still be freely available everywhere. I do not desire you for sex. However, one must still go where the food is. As you will note when you get to see my present-day girth, food may very well be number one on the McManus list of needs. So, if you are free, why don't we honor Dr. Maslow, my girth, and also see what's on your mind, at dinner tonight at my favorite eatery, the original Junior's Restaurant on Flatbush Avenue in Brooklyn. It also happens to have been Dr. Maslow's favorite when he taught at Brooklyn College in the '50's."

Connie was of course familiar with the original Juniors, as their cream cheesecake was the world standard, and he was addicted to it. It was almost, but not quite, the equivalent of Franco's passion for gelato!

He agreed to be there at 7:00.

As the meeting had a personal element to it, he gave Franco the night off.

CHAPTER 41

"Sir," Connie said, "you must be Michael McManus. Your facial features are etched into my memory and to me are absolutely unchanged. However, I will not comment on your once abundant red hair or your previously mentioned proportion of belly to height.

It is such a pleasure and honor to meet with my boyhood hero. Along with my dad, you are responsible for pointing to the road I have since taken into public service. I even open my group meetings with fellow officers with a direct quotation that I remember you imparting to that 16-year-old, little me: Protect one stranger and you will have protected your family."

"Relax, Connie, we are no longer adult and child, but fellow officers in the service of protecting our citizens.

Also, drop the sir! My name is Mike."

After about an hour of catching up on the old days, where the subsequent years had gone and personal life data, Connie got to the nub of the telephone call this morning.

He gave a history of the victim, the modus operandi of the suspect, the info culled from New York, Italy and Indianapolis. Just the very act of sharing the almost-chaotic information floating around his cerebellum helped cast some sort of order in Connie's thinking process.

Mike's interruptions to the narrative were minimal as they were both well trained in the common language used by people in their profession.

"OK, how can I help," was Mike's understanding response.

Connie answered with, "I am reasonably sure that our suspect's background is somewhere in your system. It must be, given his international activity throughout the years. I would further venture an educated guess that he is a starred Person of Interest on your international arrivals and departures watchlist. I need everything about him. Everything in your files as well as any special reports you might have on his current movements.

How does he travel? Any known associates? Known forgers of passports, visas, driver's licenses, etc. that he may have used? Sanctuaries? Rabbit holes? Aliases? Photos? Artist renderings? Cosmetic surgery? Weaponry? Special skills?

Need I go on?"

"No," Mike replied. "It is exactly what I would have asked had our places been reversed. I will get my number 2 to copy everything we have and he will hand deliver it to you.

Will tomorrow morning be soon enough?"

"Mike, you are indeed a scholar and a gentleman, as well as a continuing inspiration. You have also retained your place as my boyhood hero."

After the usual formalities of "we have to get together more often than every 20 years," the evening ended.

Mike returned to his office to inform his number 2 that he was about to pull an all-nighter.

Connie then called Lucy and said, "I can't do a thing until tomorrow morning. I am totally free for the next 12 hours. Can you think of anything I can do to fill this rare time vacuum?"

Lucy immediately responded with, "Why don't you come over so that we can put our heads, and other parts, together and work on your condom, oops, I meant to say conundrum, together."

"Will be there in about two hours."

CHAPTER 42

One hour and fifty-seven minutes later found an over-anxious Connie at Lucy's door. Their secret doorbell signal, ring-ring pause ring-ring-ring-ring (to the rhythm of a "A shave and a haircut") brought no response.

He mused, "She must be at the other end of the apartment, probably still in the shower."

Connie waited a good two minutes before ringing again.

Still no response.

Getting a little concerned he then called her cell phone.

No answer.

That's when he became really concerned and banged hard on the door.

Nothing.

Connie then remembered the spare key that Lucy had hidden under a neighbor's doormat. He found it and opened the door yelling out her name.

No response.

No one there.

His professional inner self immediately took over and he searched the apartment. There it was, on the refrigerator door.

The note.

Lt. Collins,

Lucy is my guest! No harm will come to her as long as you follow my simple instructions. You will put your investigation on a back burner. You will delay findings for two weeks to give me ample time to arrange for my departure from these shores. When I am away from your grasp you will be contacted to tell you where you can find a safe and relatively healthy Lucy. If I am caught before such time you will eventually find her assorted body parts. You will be contacted within 12 hours to be given further directions.

Your decision.

There was no time for emotion. Lt. Collins was on automatic professional response.

Personal involvement had to be placed on a back burner, except for the one promise he now made to himself: That bastard will be dead before he does any further harm.

He immediately called in the situation to his Captain for team backup.

The Captain told Connie to step down on this part of the investigation as he had too much of a personal stake in its outcome.

Connie argued, successfully, about his years of professional detachment from the cases under his lead and more specifically, his accumulated knowledge about this particular son-of-a-bitch.

He won his point and retained his lead. His inner dedicated professionalism took over without skipping a beat.

Not another moment was to be wasted as he donned the blue latex gloves, always to be found on his pants belt next to his Glock and cuffs.

Connie did a quick but thorough search while thinking ahead, "The team should be here in a matter of minutes. Forensics will scrub the premises micro-millimeter by micro-millimeter, while the rest of my team seeks witnesses and any possible input from publicly placed cameras in the area.

He followed his professional hunch and carefully followed the route to the service stairs. About mid-way down his eyes were drawn to a glint on the carpet. There it was, a pearl earring attached to a gold clip. One of the pair he had given to Lucy some two weeks ago. He then knew that she had been here and that he was indeed in the perp's mind set.

What would be his/my next step?"

In the interim, his call to the Captain was immediately re-routed to Franco, Connie's second in command. When Franco realized what was at stake, not a moment was lost.

Franco and most of the team were in Lucy's apartment within ten minutes. The remaining members who were further afield took longer—but not by much.

While forensics was busy doing its usual precision investigation, Connie spelled out individual assignments to the detectives, and they sped off. The respect and friendship that Connie had earned from his team, and all others who knew him, was enough to ensure that this was to be an absolutely super quick and precise investigation. They all knew that there was to be no sleep until the matter was positively resolved.

Positively meant the same to all involved:

No casualties and perp caught, dead or alive.

Preferably not alive!

CHAPTER 43

Within hours, forensics confirmed the handwriting to be that of Anthony Scalioni, which was further verified hours later via rapid DNA tests.

The pearl earring had Lucy's DNA traces on it. No doubt about her having been on the back stairs, a place she had always avoided as being unsafe.

They had turned up no fingerprints within the apartment other than from Lucy, Connie and Anthony. He was, as per his MO, still working alone.

Connie asked Franco to direct the now heavily reinforced squad activities and their individual assignments.

Franco's first impulse, followed by immediate action, was to look for any cameras that might have been installed in the alley. "That's what I want!" he murmured to himself. "Just across the alley, outside of the back door of the Chinese restaurant on the next parallel street."

He went inside and after much futile English requests enhanced by gestures, he found the owner, who fortunately did speak English.

Sort of.

They went to a closet in the kitchen where the tape loop for the last 24 hours was stored. He rushed it to the Precinct and had it scanned for the estimated time period, the last six hours.

There he was, a male in a baseball cap hefting a rolled carpet over his shoulder. Although the face was obscured, the athletic shape was his. No doubt about it, that was their man! He placed the carpet in the back of an SUV, closed the hatch and drove off.

The tape was given to the computer specialist who manipulated it to see if he could bring up the license plate. All they could get were some obscured letters and a number "SB 6." However, she did manage to enhance the view of a small logo on the lower left side of the hatchback door that read "Avis."

Calls were made to Avis headquarters where a team was set into action to identify the outlet that rented the car and determine the full license number, the car's make and color as well as the ID of the renter.

Several hours later, Avis called back and told Franco that the car was a 2016 blue Lexus 350 and was rented by a Jeb Thomas. All of the rental conditions and credit card specifics were spelled out. None of the personal information was important as it was all immediately checked and proved to be phony. However, the car details were broadcast to all surrounding states' police departments.

Additionally, all bridge and tunnel cameras were to be scanned to see if the car had used any of them.

While that was going on, Connie now had the time to follow his own instincts.

He found an empty office, closed and locked the door, and sat down to do some heavy solitary thinking. His thinking was in the mindset of the perp, as Connie had come to know him.

Every individual within the building immediately knew the process. Connie was not to be disturbed. All calls and other interruptions to this sacred process were to be blocked.

No interruptions.

The first thing I would have to address, Connie noted to himself, *is that right now I have all of the money and identities I need. No problem for me there. Where would I hole up with a hostage until I can leave the country?*

Secondly, I have always been a loner. I have no friends or even acquaintances. I am dependent on no one other than for the occasional re-arming supplies and ID changes. These contacts probably know nothing about me except for the ready cash that passes into their hands.

Further, since I can leave the US in any manner I deem to be safe, that is not my big problem. How will I keep this hostage alive and hidden, especially after I leave the country? After all, she is not on my hit list. I am a paid professional assassin not a casual murderer. But she is my insurance policy that provides the time for me to make the necessary departure arrangements.

Further, I cannot depend on anyone else to be her minder.

I always work solo and must make arrangements to accommodate that scenario.

The bottom line is that I need her and would prefer not to harm her. Obviously my life is more important than hers.

With those limitations, that is, Connie's version of Anthony's thought processes, he began to conceptualize the bastard's overall escape plan.

Right or wrong, it was at least a starting point.

If I were Anthony I would have thought this out in an orderly step-by-step process, Connie's racing mind further postulated.

Covert surveillance would inform me of her schedule and when she would likely be home. Gaining entry to her apartment would not be an impediment for me. I would plan to be inside her apartment just before she returns at the end of her workday. While there I would probably cut her computer lines and prepare everything necessary to surprise her, keep her quiet and controllable as well as placing the letter for that police lieutenant.

As Franco confirmed, I would carry her bound and sedated body rolled in a carpet down the three flights of usually deserted service stairs to the car parked in the rear alley near the building's service entrance.

Now what would I do next?

I'd probably drive to a very remote area where I would keep her in one of my safe houses, shackled, but within reach of food and water. The location would have to be remote enough that her screams would go unheard in the surrounding woods. There would be no need for a minder.

If I make it out of the country I would inform that Lieutenant as to where to find her. If caught, I would use her location as a bargaining chip.

At least I know they will not kill me before knowing where she is.

After going through that scenario several times and modifying it as he replayed it in his mind, it was time to take action.

Just then his solitary confinement was broken by an excited Franco who rushed into the room and almost screamed, "His car went across the Tappan Zee Bridge eight hours ago! A camera then picked him up some 20 minutes later on I-17 heading west."

Connie thanked him for the info and said, "I will be spending all of my waking hours in the foreseeable future as a bloodhound stalking this bastard. I want you as the temporary squad lead to get every available detective and street cop in New York State, New Jersey and Pennsylvania moving in a coordinated investigation.

If any stone is unturned, it's because you already viewed it from a tunnel underneath.

If any potential witness has not been thoroughly interviewed, it's because he is dead.

You are me and know exactly what I want and what is needed.

You will be thinking both inside and outside the box.

These are my initial thoughts. Need I say more?"

"No boss," Franco responded. "I'm on it! Why are *you* still here!"

CHAPTER 44

While Franco was sending information to the now greatly enhanced tri-state squad, Connie was checking rural maps in the same area.

After an initial few hours of seeking potential sites, totally isolated and in relative close proximity to New York City, he eliminated North New Jersey as being too populated to harbor a secluded area that fit his imagined conditions. There were no private rural areas large enough to support an isolated cabin that no one would just happen to come upon.

Pennsylvania and Connecticut were not a consideration because of the perp's use of the Tappan Zee Bridge, which pointed to New York State.

Connie made a conscious decision, right or wrong, to limit his search area to the Catskill Mountains. He had deduced that this was likely the closest point to meet all of the requirements needed to house Lucy, *if* his theory was correct.

That was one big If! Lucy's life was completely dependent on his intuition.

With complete police commandant support, Connie boarded a city-owned helicopter at Pier 46, at its home pad just adjacent to the Hudson River. One hour later, they landed in Albany on a restricted pad at the periphery of the New York State government center. The copter and pilot were provided for his exclusive use for whatever period of time he deemed necessary.

After several false starts into the wrong buildings, Connie found the home of the Department of Interior for the State of New York.

While Connie was in flight to Albany, telephone calls by the Commissioner of Police in New York City directly to the New York State Secretary of the Interior cleared his way to immediate assistance.

He was expected.

Departmental cartographers were already at work poring over segmented maps, seeking areas within or near the Catskill Mountains that would meet Connie's parameters. By the time he was introduced to the three team members, they had initial findings to go over with him.

Totally rural areas, miles away from any semblance of civilization, were highlighted for him, complete with aerial photo streams for his review.

During the chopper flight Connie had time to redefine the list of requirements that he felt would be necessary to support the imprisonment theory he had imagined.

1. It had to be far off the beaten track. At least five to ten miles from the nearest neighbor or tertiary road.
2. No power, telephone or other service lines would be available.
3. No roads. Not even a rudimentary rough track. A primitive trail would likely have to be negotiated using some form of motorized jungle buggy. This was considered a necessity by Connie because of the need to transport the weight of the victim and life sustaining supplies for a two-week period over that distance.
4. No more than a simple one-room, probably windowless, shack.
5. Enough ground vegetation and tall trees to ensure total isolation from prying eyes, both on the ground and in the sky.

These requirements were discussed in some detail with the three experts to help them define and further refine their search parameters.

While this was in progress, contacts escalating from the Mayor of New York City to the Governor of the State to the Commandant of the Eastern Region of the US Air Force were underway. A specially re-fitted Boeing 737 jet with ground imaging capability was flown from its California home base to Stewart Air Force Base, near Newburgh, New York, conveniently located at the southeastern base of the Catskill Mountains.

Ground imaging, an offshoot of radar, was developed by the military and had the capability to "see" what was on the ground by penetrating through absolute darkness, vegetation, fog, mist, etc.

The aft section of this flying laboratory, where the bulk of the passengers would normally be seated in coach, was dedicated to all of the technical equipment needed for this unique type of operation. The forward section was occupied by the flight crew in the cockpit and the First Class section behind them crammed with technicians, computers and screens. These were the specialists doing the job that this entire machine was dedicated to: ground imaging.

After several hours and 4,286 cups of coffee (or some other number not even remotely close to that), the team agreed on several areas that justified further examination.

It was time for the four of them to gather their maps, courage and coffee mugs to board the waiting chopper for the quick flight from Albany to Stewart AFB. The noisy and amusement park-like bouncy flight did not stop them from using the time to once again redefine and zero in on the likely target areas for the air search.

They were driven directly from the chopper's landing pad to the waiting jet. It was like leaving the shack they were now seeking to being ushered into the Governor's mansion.

The portable stairs had been rolled up to the plane's open front door and the four-man team climbed up. We have often seen the President of the United States make a similar ascent boarding Air Force 1, but that was a Jumbo jet. He walked up three stories without any visible exertion. The difference was that the President never seemed to be winded. Connie, on the other hand was panting by the time he reached the plane's single story door.

So much for his almost-weekly visit to the gym.

They were assigned seats facing a giant LED screen that mimicked the smaller one that the lead tech, Lt. Grafton, was seated in front of. The difference between the two screens, other than obvious size, was that Grafton controlled the apparatus. Connie and his cartographers were only observers.

In addition to the three cartographers who had accompanied Connie, by arrangement made before leaving Albany, a State Forest Ranger, Len

Deston, familiar with the terrain they were to be observing, was flown in from the Monticello area. He would be the most familiar with ground conditions in any areas of potential interest.

All of the crew and guests were linked by individual audio headsets for real time communication. There would be zero time lag between suggested flight variations and/or imaging adjustments.

The stairs were rolled back, the door closed and seat belts fastened.

CHAPTER 45

The plane had a dedicated chart viewing area set aside in of the front of the cabin. It was positioned in close proximity to the cockpit for the convenience and availability of the Captain during course deviation discussions while in flight.

Captain Lorstan, Lt. Grafton and the five civilians were gathered around a pull-out flat table with a pile of maps brought by the cartographers.

After the usual courtesy introductions, Captain Lorstan, a man of few words but great aviation skills, tersely addressed Connie, "OK, sir, where am I taking you to?"

Connie, after their final agreement on the chopper and as the leader of this exploratory expedition, replied as he unfolded map number 1, "This area marked in red is part of the National Preserve and seems to have all of the conditions we deemed necessary for the isolated confinement of the person of interest that we are looking for."

Further details were not necessary for the group to know for the purpose of this mission, and Connie chose to be silent on the details other than that an important life was very much dependent on the success of their reconnaissance.

As professionals in their chosen careers, that was all they wanted or needed to know. They were just eager to get started.

Connie again pointed to the area within the red outline on the map, noted as Sector A, and said, "This is where I suggest we begin. It is some

300 square miles of isolated, mountainous and heavily forested land. There are no known settlements, roads, trails or dwellings. All of those were specifically banned by the U.S. National Preserve Act of 1906.

The purpose of this mission is to see if, despite the Act, there is some sort of shack or other form of habitat hidden amongst the tall trees and dense ground vegetation. If so, we will further investigate on the ground. If not, we will go on to area number two.

Captain, what is your estimate of the flight time required to cover the complete Sector A?"

Captain Lorstan did a quick mental calculation and replied, "My guestimate, based on a grid sweep with five-mile-wide coverage, is about one hour."

"OK, Captain, let's get this monster moving."

Within about 15 minutes of wheels up, a voice interrupted the monotony of the drone of the engine's constant hum invading all headsets, "This is the Captain. We are now entering the southeast corner of the red outlined sector on your map number 1. We are heading due north and should reach the northeastern terminus of this first leg in 17 minutes."

All eyes in the cabin focused on either the individual dedicated screens at their workstations or on the large one facing Connie and his contingent. A serene but moving image of an unbroken expanse of lush green treetops covered the screens. Every so often almost-recognizable images hidden by the treetops would appear as distinct shadow outlines captured in subtle gray tones by the imaging cameras. Lt. Grafton used his experience to interpret these particular images as meandering streams or rocky ridges.

For the next twenty minutes, the screens were a monotonous green, interrupted every so often by other gray shapes identified as rivulets, ponds and bounding animals.

"Whoa!" Connie yelled. "What is that?"

There was the distinct outline of two adjacent straight-sided rectangular objects that could only be manmade and had to be parts of some sort of structure. Nature rarely provided absolutely straight lines.

Captain Lorstan immediately responded to Connie's ear-blasting yell and announced that he had already entered the coordinates of their find and could return at a lower altitude for finer contrast imaging.

However, Forest Ranger Len interrupted and said, "I know this building. If you look to the right you can see the outline of a relatively navigable small river occasionally used by local fishermen. They call the river "The Trout," for obvious reasons. The shack was erected about 75 years ago for the locals' convenience, and is used by them on an infrequent basis, but often enough that it would not be suitable for the purpose you have proposed.

It is a known and used area that has much too easy access.

I sincerely doubt that it would be what you are looking for."

Connie thanked him for his input and asked the Captain to continue on course.

The craft flew the remainder of the first sector and two more without ID-ing any potential sites.

Strained eyes were beginning to tire when about midway through the final sector pass Connie got up to stretch his legs. Almost immediately he heard another "Whoa!" This time it was from Len.

"That looks like the outline of another man-made structure, there on the lower right, and I am definitely not familiar with it."

Captain Lorstan immediately confirmed, noting the coordinates of the object.

Connie asked him if they could do another fly-over and fine-tune the screen's clarity of the object.

Lt. Grafton gave detailed instructions to his imaging techs as the plane gracefully swooped in a broad 360-degree correction to its course. At the same time, the Captain slowed the air speed to 312 mph, the slowest he could fly without stalling.

In the cabin behind, dials were turned and new instructions entered into computers. The screens immediately showed a smaller area and when the coordinates were confirmed, what had been small gray shadows became more sharply defined black and much-larger objects. Even Connie could now see the difference between rock formations, ground level brush and the subject's very rectangular shape.

High-resolution cameras were now capturing the changing terrain below. As they passed over this area of interest it became more apparent that there was some sort of freestanding cabin below. They were even able to make out a winding path leading up to it that was just wide enough to accommodate a small all-terrain vehicle.

Connie requested that the remainder of the trip be put on hold and that they return to base. At the same time, calls were made to the helicopter pilot to be on standby for their return. New York State Police were alerted and asked to accompany Connie on the chopper and in a second one, as backup. That second chopper was requested to have an all-terrain vehicle on board.

He also left instructions for the Captain and crew, including the cartographers, to then fly back to the last coordinates and continue the search after he disembarked. Should this first site be unproductive at least the search was ongoing.

Len, the Forest Ranger, would accompany Connie and the ground search party.

Captain Lorstan radioed the subject cabin's coordinates to the chopper pilots as Connie and Len disembarked.

A waiting van transported the two to the idling chopper. As soon as they were aboard and strapped in, it took off.

No time was to be lost.

CHAPTER 46

Connie suggested that the pilots find a landing site at least one mile from the cabin so as not to forewarn the occupant(s). In no event was there to be a direct flyover. That would be dead giveaway! You know what I mean.

Because they were flying a direct route, as opposed to the sector search that the much faster jet took, the flying time was actually about the same as the jet's to reach the area in question.

They scanned the area from about five miles from the cabin coordinates at an altitude of about 1,000 feet to see if there were any breaks in the trees that would allow them to land.

"There!" the pilot said. "On the left there is a clearing that appears to be large enough for us. I estimate it to be about 1-1/2 to 2 miles from the cabin."

"Go for it. Please keep us as low as you can safely approach the landing site so as to limit the area covered by chopper noise," was Connie's immediate response.

As the chopper was touching down, Connie and three back-up state police officers jumped to the ground and without looking back, started to race in the direction of the cabin.

After twenty minutes, the cabin was in sight through the dense surrounding brush. Using hand signals only, the four of them circled in different courses so that their final approach would surround the cabin.

This took an additional five minutes. Prearranged double clicks in their ear buds was the signal to silently approach the cabin, stopping just behind the brush some ten feet from the cabin.

A triple click by Connie was the final signal. The four of them rushed the cabin with weapons drawn. Connie had a ram in hand and battered down the door. He rushed in screaming at top voice, "Police! Hands in the air!" The three others crashed through windows almost simultaneously, also screaming, "Police."

The four of them disappointedly faced only each other in an otherwise empty house full of cobwebs, rodent droppings, dirt floor and a small pool of water under the hole in the roof. This cabin obviously had been unoccupied for many, many years.

Connie, in his professional experience, was used to following unsuccessful leads and without interruption, continued the investigation. He immediately contacted the chopper pilot and gave him detailed instructions. In order to save time, he was to take one of the all-terrain vehicles and pick them up. Before leaving he was to contact the jet captain and fill him in and pass on instructions to continue the search.

What Connie was not aware of was that the imaging crew had already found yet another set of black lines identified in a subsequent second pass as a cabin.

It was but 90 miles from Connie's current location.

Within 30 minutes, the chopper was back in the air heading towards the second sighting, just a ten-minute flight time away.

The same protocol was in place, with the chopper landing in a small clearing an estimated one mile from the cabin.

While still about two feet from touchdown, Connie and his three police backup jumped to the ground, got their bearings and started at a fast pace toward the cabin.

Using the same approach procedure, they stopped in the bush about fifty feet from the now visible cabin. The three State Police officers continued around, one to the rear and the other two to each of the sides. When all were in place as designated by the single click in their ear buds, they were ready for the incursion.

On hearing Connie's triple click, with weapons at the ready the three simultaneously crashed through windows as Connie, once again, battered the front door in.

It was immediately apparent that there was only one occupant in the room, and she posed no threat.

Lying on the floor in the middle of the room was a very pale and visibly shaken woman. Connie ran directly to her and embraced her in a bear hug of joy that could have been more injurious than anything she had gone through to date.

Happiness trumped ordeal!

While this intimate moment was going on, the three officers scouted the area to make sure there were no traps or naughty guys hanging around.

After the long hug, Connie checked for traps within the cabin and using standard police keys, opened the handcuffs connecting Lucy's left ankle to a chain tether. The tether, in one unbroken circle was wrapped around a central steel column in the middle of the room. The diameter of the circle was large enough for Lucy to reach a cache of food and a large bucket that was used as her privy.

The entire arrangement was as he had imagined. It wasn't magic, voodoo or dumb luck. Connie was once again able to think like the perp, as he had so often done in his very successful police career.

For the first time in his memory, Connie actually shed tears of joy. They were a mere few drops in comparison to the tsunami emitting from Lucy and even the three hardened police officers.

Once back at Stewart Air Force Base, Lucy was given a thorough examination by the Base's medical staff and given a relatively clean bill of health, considering the ordeal she had just gone through.

Connie looked into Lucy's eyes and said, "I will catch this son of a bitch and make sure that he pays for what he has done to you."

CHAPTER 47

Back to the original quest.

A quick snooze in one of the empty holding cells, followed by cold water slapped on the face, a mouth rinse, an electric shave and a cup of the black stuff that had been sitting on the hot plate all night was all that Connie needed to face the horde the next morning. As he always did on these occasions, he mused, *Why don't I learn to use that electric shaver at home instead of that scar-inducing, blunt blade I use and reuse, and reuse?*

And as usual, when at home, he would revert to his old bad habits resulting in the toilet paper covering routine. At least at home he could brush his teeth and the coffee was almost better than at the Precinct.

He got to his desk just as some unknown young, well-built suit walked in and asked Franco for Detective Lieutenant Collins. He was directed to Connie's desk and presented his credentials as he identified himself as Special Agent Derek Marlin of the Department of Homeland Security.

Connie stood up, smiled and shook hands while saying, "Derek, good to meet you. I've been expecting you. You must work with Mike."

"Sir, I do work for Director McManus, and he has told me a great deal about you and your famed dad. It is a true pleasure to meet you."

He opened his briefcase and removed a three-inch pile of papers. "These are copies of all of the files that we have on the individual that you requested. The Director also asked me to spend as much time as you deem necessary to answer any questions that might arise during your perusal of same."

"Thank you for what must have been an all-nighter on your part in pulling this together, and for the kind offer of assistance. We really appreciate this cooperation. Franco, the tall lug you first spoke to, will be responsible for combing through the info you brought.

Let's go to his desk for a proper introduction."

After getting them started, Connie returned to his corner of the world, sat down next to his third-best friend, his phone, and called his first best friend, Lucy.

Yeah, it had gotten even more serious in just one month.

Arrangements were made for dinner that night at his place, with dessert to be served at her place.

"See ya later."

When the image of her and her recent ordeal finally dissolved, the puce walls of the squad room began to reenter his consciousness, and recognition returned that he still had a murderer to catch.

Puce=Murder? Just in my head, as Connie dismissed the invading thought.

After fielding several calls from his various detectives with questions about leads, turf, egos, limits, law, donuts, etc., he started on his own line of inquiry. But first, with his second-best friend in hand (and his first-best to be in that position later), he called Mike to thank him for a great dinner and of course his rapid response to the request for info. They also again vowed to keep in touch more often than once every twenty years.

As he was about to place the next call, Franco's phone rang at his now empty desk. With Franco away for the moment, Connie ran over, picked up the phone and punched in Franco's extension. The greeting at the other end was not that of an English speaker, but very definitely had an Italian accent.

"Allo. Is this Franco?"

"No, Franco stepped away from his desk. This is Lieutenant Collins. Can I help you?"

"Si, I am familiar with your name from the daily calls that Franco placed to you during his most welcome stay in Italy. This is Detective Laticco, Commandant of the special squad investigating the possible role of the Prince in your ongoing murder investigation."

Connie responded, "Yes, Commodore Laticco, of course I know who you are and would like to extend my personal gratitude to you on the extremely efficient and professional manner in which you and your group approached and resolved the problem we handed to you. It was a magnificent, expedited and extremely professional investigation with very positive results. We can't thank you enough."

"That is very kind of you to say and I will be sure to pass your comments to my team. However, we are not finished, as we have uncovered some new information that might prove to be helpful to you in locating the suspect you have been seeking. We have been poring through a vanload of papers collected from the Prince's residences and offices, as well as those of his lawyers and accountants. In one of his accountant's files we noted a transfer of two million dollars to an account number in an American bank just last week. This was particularly suspicious because it was signed by the Prince, who had been dead for at least two months. The transfer had no details other than the number."

Laticco then gave Connie the name of the bank and the account number.

After again thanking him for his professionalism, his diligence in the pursuit of this important information, and lastly, his kind hospitality to Franco during his recent visit to Italy, he then extended an invitation for him to visit New York to attend the booking of the suspect.

Franco walked into the squad room just before the conversation had ended and managed to say hello to his new friend, and once again also thank him.

Connie filled Franco in on the essence of the phone conversation.

"Franco, please dig up the location and the name of the responsible officer of the bank. Not just a local title, but someone who can really help us. Arrange an appointment for us to be there right after lunch."

A week of scrumptious Italian food interspersed with gelato followed by gelato, etc., did not seem to have slowed him down, as Franco dashed out the door.

Connie yelled across the room to Detective Boyer who was a top-notch detective and as a special bonus to all in the room, looked nothing like a "boy"- er, "Please chase down all remittances from Italy to the bank over the last six months."

Her immediate response was, "On it sir."

CHAPTER 48

The nameplate on the solid oak door said:

> *Thomas J. Horton, Executive Vice President*
> *First US International Bank*

The immaculately clad and trim man behind the desk looked exactly like Tommy Horton should look: Commodore of the Marina Fleet, Captain of the Club Polo Team and past champion of the Eastern Division Men's Singles Tennis Tourney. At least that was the aura he exuded.

Incidentally, he also seemed to be quite intelligent.

Horton fit the job description for his responsibilities as Executive VP and was obviously the bank honcho they needed to talk to.

"Good job, Franco."

After the necessary introductory pleasantries, Connie got down to brass tacks. In this environment, they should have been solid gold tacks.

"Mr. Horton, we are here on a very delicate mission. Our entire conversation is covered by the Official Secrets Act and must remain privy to you and you alone within and outside of this bank. Basically, we are desperate to catch a major professional assassin who has been responsible for the murder of a large number of major international government and corporate officials around the world. Our specific involvement has been necessitated by the recent murder of a US citizen, with international implications."

Connie continued, "We are aware of a recent international banking transaction that involved the transfer of some two million dollars from the Banco Roma to your institution. All we have is the transaction number and the date."

He then passed his scribbled copy of same across the desk to Horton, who started to type the information into his computer.

He was not just a pretty face, but actually knew how to get things done.

After a series of additional typing inputs, yes, he even remembered his passwords, he smiled and uttered, "Gotcha!" Even the Hortons are familiar with the street lingo.

He looked up and said, "The money came in last Tuesday and cleared immediately as Prince Emanuel II is a well-known customer of ours, and yes he was the remitter of the funds. The recipient, who picked up the money in cash that very same afternoon, was one Mr. Harry Sands. As he was not known to us, he was required to supply the correct password. It was provided by him, which allowed the completion of the transfer."

Connie interrupted, "Can we assume you have a photograph of the transaction?"

"Of course." Horton continue, "It is standard procedure on all Bank transactions. I will have my Tech Support group retrieve a copy for you. It should not take more than a few minutes."

While waiting for the photo, they continued their conversation. The address and telephone number supplied to contact Mr. Sands was that of the Marriott Marquis on Broadway. Connie noted it and immediately called his office to get a team there ASAP to seal off the room and any records of Mr. Sands' visit.

As promised, a beard (obviously a Techie) knocked on the door and entered with the photograph of the recipient. No surprise. It was the suspect, complete with red beard, red hair and glasses.

This was the first solid proof of his involvement in the murder.

Connie thanked Mr. Horton for all of his help and he and Franco took their leave.

Connie now had to build on what they had just learned in order to find the son of a bitch before he left the country, if it was not too late already.

"Come on, Franco, let's get to the Marriott."

CHAPTER 49

"Yes, the Resident General Manager," repeated Connie. "I need to speak to him now, not tomorrow, not next week, NOW! Am I getting through to you or do we have to shut the entire hotel down? NOW!"

The deliciously plump, semi-attractive, quasi-redhead of undetermined age understood. Ms. Francis had her Executive Assistant job because she could process input and immediately come to the same executive decision her boss would have made.

NOW obviously meant NOW.

"Yes, sir, I understand NOW and will get Mr. Dunn out of his important meeting with Mr. Marriott right now. Can I come to work for you when he fires me?"

Connie smiled and said, "I can assure you, ma'am, that this is a truly major matter and you will not be fired. Should that happen, I will personally put Mr. Marriott behind bars unless he gives you Mr. Dunn's job.

Now let's go."

They scooted through the rear door of the office, which led directly into the conference room. There were Dunn and all of his department managers seated around the conference table. All eyes were riveted on their revered, really big boss as he congratulated them on being awarded the first-place trophy for being the best something-or-other in their renowned international group of hotels.

The unannounced intrusion into this holy sanctuary caused an almost audible click of eighteen eyeballs as they turned in unison to the door.

The normally sanguine Dunn turned red, stood up and demanded to know what this was all about.

A bewildered Mr. Marriott at the head of the table retained his composure.

He was probably very used to boardroom battles.

A very few seconds later Connie said to Mr. Marriott, "I am indeed sorry for this interruption of your important and private meeting. My name and title is Lieutenant Collins and this is Detective Sergeant DiAngelo of the New York City Police Department, and we are here on a matter of extreme urgency. I can immediately assure you that this hotel and its staff are not part of the problem, but we do need your assistance. May I ask that all, other than Mr. Marriott and Mr Dunn, leave the room?"

When the others were gone, Connie continued, "Gentlemen, again I ask your forgiveness for this rude interruption of your meeting, but we are on a severe time restraint."

He then related the background information about the murder of Enrico Calzoni, the probable involvement of the late Prince Emanuel II of Italy and his close associates, and finally the suspect that they were now seeking.

"He is an international assassin wanted not only by the US but most European and Asian governments as well. We must catch him before he leaves the USA, if he has not already done so. This is where we need your assistance. His last known residence was at this property, and we need to know where he went from here. I assure you that our presence here and any help that you may be able to provide will remain absolutely private and will not be shared with others in the Police Department, Federal Agents, foreign governments and most certainly not the public. The fine Marriott pristine image will not be tainted."

Both hoteliers were stunned and could not believe that they were so essential to a murder investigation, especially one of this magnitude. This sort of thing just does not happen in, or even near their vast number of Marriott properties.

"What is it we can do assist you?" asked Mr. Marriott.

"We need your assistance in combing through your records over the last few weeks. We have a picture of the suspect but do not know what name he may have used. We will need to question your staff to see if anyone recognizes him. Hopefully that will yield a name. The name could then reveal when he checked out. If so, we can go deeper and see if there were any visitors, telephone calls, credit cards used, reservations made, etc. Your records could possibly give us the leads we so desperately need to apprehend him—or not. Either way, this is the only course open to us at this time.

With your agreement, as a first step, we would like to start questioning your staff now. We will not tell them the reason for the search, so as to maintain the confidentiality of your hotel's involvement. Do you have any objections or suggestions?"

A simultaneous nod of both heads indicated their agreement with the go-ahead.

CHAPTER 50

A general briefing, avoiding mention of the reason behind the needed information while still stressing confidentiality, opened their meeting with the assembled group of department heads. All of them were represented from housekeeping to front desk, from custodial to food and beverage, and porters to back room.

They were told to immediately deploy their staff to look at the photo of the suspect, go over all records. The need for information regarding auto rental and flight reservations was paramount. They were told that anything they might recall could be of significance and not to hold anything back.

After Connie thanked them, they scurried to their respective areas to scour their records and their memories.

Connie and Franco remained in the conference room, which was set up as their temporary War Room. The General Manager provided an urn of coffee, sandwiches and a direct outside telephone line and then left the detectives in privacy. Dunn's parting words were, "I am at your disposal and will remain available until you have completed this part of your investigation."

It was not more than twenty minutes later when there was a gentle knock on the door.

Connie yelled, "Come in!"

A twenty-something petite brunette in a black beribboned Marriott room-maid's smock entered and introduced herself, in a Latino accent, as Consuella.

Connie invited her to help herself to a coffee and snack and to take a seat. She was obviously nervous. Connie figured that she had to be a documented worker in order to have a job with a major group like Marriott, so that was not likely the source of her anxiety. After a few minutes of the usual chitchat, where are you originally from? how do you like your new life? do you like your job? etc., Connie finally understood the source of her anxiety. This was the first time she had ever actually met an American policeman and she did not know what to expect. He realized what he would have to do in subsequent interviews to put the employees at ease.

"Please, Consuella, take your time and tell us what information you have that could help us in our investigation. Keep in mind that any little detail you bring to us could be very important in the capture of a very dangerous man. Your participation and valuable information will be treated with absolute confidentiality and never be revealed to anyone else. So please let us know why you are here."

Consuella feebly tried to smile, sat upright, straightened her apron and finally said, "I recognized the man in the picture my manager showed me and he urged me to come see you."

Connie prompted her with a sweep of his arm to continue.

"The man was in room 762 for almost a week and finally left this morning. I remember him for two reasons. He left an envelope with my name on it containing a thank-you note and a ten-dollar bill. People rarely take the time to do that in business hotels. The second reason was that after he left I found a set of keys under the stuffed chair cushion. It had to be his because that chair, along with the rest of the room, is thoroughly cleaned every day, and it had not been there before. I gave the keys to my Manager, Miss Diaz."

"What did you do with the note he left you?"

She thought for a second, and then responded, "After removing the ten-dollar bill, I had no need for the note and threw it in the trash."

"No problem. That is what I probably would have done. Anything else you remember?" Connie asked.

After a minute of thinking, Consuella responded in the negative.

Murder at the Met

"Consuella, you have been extremely helpful and we wish to thank you. If ever you need some help or advice, we would be pleased to return the favor. You have two friends at the New York Police Department."

A tentatively smiling Consuella rose from her chair, nodded, and left the room.

Franco grinned and said, "The vital keystone that could help us unlock the rest of this puzzle."

Connie picked up the phone and asked for Miss Diaz to come to the conference room.

"The door is unlocked, please come in!" Connie shouted. A smartly dressed, very attractive woman of some fifty years entered and introduced herself as Henrietta Diaz, Housekeeping Manager.

"Miss Diaz, we would like to first emphasize that we have asked you to join us this morning to help us with a very nasty problem we are working on. You, and your staff, are in no way under investigation or suspicion for anything. We just really appreciate you being here and helping us with this important problem we have. Your assistance could be vital in helping us to apprehend a very dangerous criminal."

There was an audible sigh of relief and a hint of a smile appeared on her face. Up to this point, her most pressing problem had been the businessman who urgently needed his rain-soaked suit pressed for an important meeting.

"How can I help you, sir?"

Connie told her about the information that Consuella had imparted, and asked about the keys she had found.

"Oh yes, I remember them. I tagged them with the date, room number and occupant's name and put them in the lost and found locker in the General Manager's office. They should be there now, as we generally keep such items for six months before either trashing them, or if of use, providing them with a new home. I can get them for you if you so desire."

"Please do so, Miss Diaz. We need to check them to see where they might lead us."

With that, she excused herself, said, "I will be back in three minutes," and went directly to her boss's office to retrieve the keys.

During that three-minute period, Franco called for the Front Desk Manager to come to the conference room. He arrived some five minutes after Miss Diaz's return with the keys. In that five-minute period, Connie managed to send the keys with a patrolman back to the station for identification.

Connie gave the same opening spiel to Felix Carter, the Front Desk Manager, that he had given to Miss Diaz. Carter was an alert young man who emitted the self-confident aura of someone destined to rise in the Marriott ranks. He was impeccably dressed and carried himself with an air of confidence. At age 25, with a Cornell degree in Hotel Management, he was well on his way.

"I was not on duty when the gentleman you described checked in, but as he was in residence for six nights, I did see him on occasion and interacted with him several times. The only difference from your description was that he had blond wavy hair and the wisp of a blond chin beard. However, I do know faces and am reasonably sure that he was the one you expressed interest in."

Connie asked, "Were there any other features that you noticed to help us in our quest?"

"Well, yes, sir," Carter responded. "He was quite muscular, but seemed to try to hide his build under loose fitting clothing. I am something of a bodybuilding nut myself and can recognize the same in others. I even noticed him several times, at odd hours, working out in our exercise room."

Connie then asked, "Did he have any special requests?"

"No, sir. To my knowledge he never ate in his room. I believe he took most of his meals locally at Friday's or Maggiano's. He breakfasted at the Cracker Barrel down the street. I know about this because I sometimes stop by the Cracker Barrel for some of their delicious pecan pancakes before my early shift. He always had a plate of fruit, yogurt and granola on his table. I recognized him as one of our guests, but he did not recognize me at that time because I jog to the hotel every morning and was dressed in my workout sweats before changing into the suit that I keep at work.

Before coming in here to see you, I checked his bill to see if there was anything special on it. The only thing was laundry on the next-to-last day he stayed with us. There were no telephone calls. Not even local ones."

"How did he settle his bill?" Connie asked.

"Our record shows cash. Just before coming in here, in anticipation of this question, I asked the clerk who was on duty the morning he checked out about his method of payment. She remembered him because he paid with twelve crisp new $100 dollar bills. As per procedure, she verified authenticity under the UV light.

He left no forwarding address.

Also, in anticipation of your next question, I made a copy of the address in Santa Fe he gave us at check-in. I am sure it is phony because I was born and raised in Santa Fe and know that there is no Ratzinger Street. I have also made a copy of the American Express card that he used at check-in."

"You are very thorough, Mr. Carter, as you asked yourself all of the right questions. Would you like a job on the force?"

"No thank you, sir. It might slow down my plan to become CEO of the Marriott Corporation within fifteen years, but I appreciate the compliment."

There was no doubt in Connie's mind that one day in the not too distant future he would see Carter's name, in bold print, in the Wall Street Journal.

As Carter was leaving the conference room, Connie's cellphone silently vibrated.

"Good morning Captain, what can I do for you?"

"I just fielded a call on your behalf from a Commodore Laticco in Rome," said the Captain. "He indicated that they were wrapping up the Italian end of the case and would appreciate if Franco could return ASAP. I hope that you are in agreement, as I've already committed that Franco would be on the redeye tonight."

"Thanks, Captain. If you could direct my secretary to arrange for tickets and a hotel, I will tell Franco that it is gelato time again. I'm quite sure there will be no grumbling on his part.

See you back at the station."

After a transfer of the call to Franco's extension, Connie said, "Franco get your ass in gear and take my car home to pack a bag. You are being booked on the 8:00 pm Alitalia flight to Rome tonight. Drop my car off at the station when you pick up your tickets. On your way, out, send the uniform on duty in the parking lot in to see me.

So, why are you still there?"

As Franco scooted out, Connie once again sat down at the conference table to review his notes. Within a few minutes there was a knock on the door.

"You wanted to see me, sir? My name is Patrolman Davis."

"I remember you, Davis, from the Toskin murder nine months ago. You took the initiative to look for and eventually found the murder weapon. As I recall, it was a chef's knife hidden in a trash bin just a few blocks away from the scene. It was the critical piece of evidence that helped put a very nasty guy behind bars for a very long time. That was well done on your part."

"Thank you, sir."

Connie continued, "I am short staffed at the moment and could use your help and intuition. Help me once again and I am sure that you will be on the short path to a promotion to the division where you will be using the uniform only for ceremonial purposes."

"I am at your command. You name it, sir."

"OK, Davis, I need you to round up all of the security tape recordings during the period that our perp was in residence here. Do this for the hotel as well as from the nearby Maggiano's, Friday's and Cracker Barrel restaurants. Don't forget their parking lots and all nearby street surveillance cameras. You are on your own, so show me some of that same initiative you so aptly displayed nine months ago.

Go!"

Connie then returned his attention to the hotel records.

A good starting point would normally be tracing credit cards that were used. Unfortunately, all of the records showed cash payments for everything.

No plastic, no paper/internet trail!

This guy is one smart cookie. He's obviously been around the block a few times and covers his back—almost surgically. It's time for me to use a scalpel and peel back some of his protective layers.

The vibration on his cellphone interrupted his stream of thought.

"Lieutenant Collins."

"Hi, Lieutenant, this is Ozzie. I traced that key you sent back to a locker in the YMCA on 126th Street. I contacted Judge Winnick, was issued a warrant, and I immediately paid a visit.

It contained a complete change of men's clothing, a red wig, horn-rimmed glasses (with clear glass lenses) and $5,000 in $100 bills. I just dropped it all off at forensics to see if they could dig up anything useful in the lot."

"Thanks, Ozzie. Keep me posted."

CHAPTER 51

There, standing at the terminal end of the arrivals ramp of Alitalia 554, was a smiling Commodore Laticco.

"Franco, welcome back to Italy! As you can see, I took the liberty of inviting your Roman mistress to greet you, the Contessa Stracciatella Gelato," as he handed over a paper cup.

The glowing smile on Franco's face lit up the entire concourse. The intensity of the glow heightened with each bite until the licked-clean empty container was discarded. The cup's former inhabitant, Stracciatella to her friends, went on a totally different personal track.

While his driver negotiated the impossibly crowded road from the airport to Central Rome, Laticco briefed Franco on the current situation in Italy, vis-a-vis the Italian connection to the New York murder, and why it was necessary for him to come back so soon.

Laticco explained, "We have made substantial progress since you left. Forget the jokes, it was not because you left. The case is essentially tied up with a neat bow and ready to be handed over to you for final justice in the USA."

"Your team really works fast," interjected Franco.

"Yes," continued Laticco. "When the breaks come our way, we run with them, and they did come our way.

Ah, after only two hours on that parking lot called the autoroute, we have finally arrived at the office.

Let's continue this briefing inside."

They drove into the garage entrance of the headquarters building and went directly up to the third-floor conference room. Awaiting them were several of Laticco's key staff as well as representatives of the various Government bureaus that were privy to the investigation. All of them were in various stages of imbibing their morning espresso and were obviously in a good mood.

After greetings to those Franco knew and introductions to the ones he had not met before, Laticco continued, "As you will soon see, we did not go to sleep after you left last week. We added forensic financial analysts to the team and really delved into the piles of records that our teams had uncovered. At the same time, there were deep interrogations of the three suspects.

The good doctor was the first to break.

After some sixteen hours of continuous probing and veiled threats, he finally admitted his role in the great deception.

Apparently, just prior to his natural demise three months ago, the Prince had stated to his trusted aide and to his financial advisor that he was aware of the existence of a legal heir to his grandfather's estate. The total value of the estate was so staggering that the Prince decided not to contest the other heir's claim. There was more than enough money to be divided. He could not envision a difference between having an additional two billion or four billion dollars added to his own current worth, which was much more than significant on its own. His attitude was especially true because of his own deteriorating health and his own lack of a legal heir.

His three most trusted confidants obviously disagreed with the Prince's plans and secretly met to devise one that would see to their own futures.

Since they were the only ones privy to the good Prince's thoughts on this matter, upon his demise, they immediately set their plan into action."

Lattico continued, "Incidentally, when faced with the doctor's confession, all of this was then separately corroborated by the other two conspirators."

"You guys don't waste any time," Franco interjected.

Laticco continued, "Now for the juicy part, the reason we asked for you to visit us so quickly. No, not just because we know you missed the

Montepulciano d'Abruzzo wine, but because of the second part of their confession.

We have a signed confession (after first reading them their Miranda rights as required in the USA), backed by the interrogation tapes, confessing the details of their elaborate plan to do the following:

First, they maintained the Prince's natural death a secret only known to the three of them. The doctor created the illusion that he was still treating his patient in a locked bedroom, accessible only by the three of them. The financial advisor forged papers changing the Prince's will to benefit the three of them. He worked closely with the Prince's unwitting lawyer, who was not involved in their crime. The personal assistant was the one who arranged for his contacts in the USA to eliminate any other potential heirs. The other two agreed with this plan."

Franco was absolutely stunned. "All of this only since my departure last week?"

Laticco responded, "Yes, and that is why we asked for you to return. The greater crime is not the fraud, but obviously their role in a murder in the USA. That is your province, and we feel that it would be appropriate for them to face the murder charges in the States first. Should they be found guilty, serve time and ultimately be released from said confinement at some much later date, we can then ask for their return to Italy to face the lesser charges here. In any event, they will not be enjoying fine dining for most, if not the rest of their lives.

Toward that end, we have arranged for their transportation in an Italian military jet tomorrow. All of the papers have been prepared and they will be in your official custody assisted by three of my men who will accompany you to help ensure a safe journey."

"On behalf of the New York Police Department, I officially accept responsibility for the three accused and wish to thank you, your exceptional Department and the government of Italy for your role in this important case.

Additionally, I would like to invite you and your core group to be my guest at a restaurant of your choice to celebrate tonight.

Wait until our police accountant sees the cost of taxis in Rome!

Now I have to call my boss in NYC."

"Yeah, Franco, why did you have to be there?" was Connie's terse answer to the ID on the caller's cell phone. "Give me a quick fill-in."

Franco then brought Connie up to date on the latest from Rome. He also got absolute approval from his boss to host the dinner that evening, but only if it started with Scampi Montuosa, included Montepulciano d' Abruzzo and ended with gelato, preferably stracciatella. The only other proviso was that he had to return with at least six bottles of Prosecco for the squad's celebration.

"Si, Signiori Lieutenant, see you tomorrow. Please have the appropriate transport available at the airport for our unwilling guests and a limo for me and my compadres."

That evening was long remembered as a blur of vino, scampi, vino, calamari, vino, fettucine amatriciana, vino, jokes (Who was that perp I saw you with last night? That was no perp, that was my mother-in-law), vino, olives, vino, grilled lamb, vino, and, of course, gelato. The team's night out was then capped with grappa and hugs and thank you, again and again.

The next morning, Franco and his accompanying detectives flew out with their three perps suitably restrained for the long flight to JFK. The bad guys were in a cell-like section of the military jet. The good guys were still flying about fifty feet above the plane when it finally landed some eight hours later.

CHAPTER 52

The three suspects were transported to separate holding cells at the lower Manhattan Courthouse, booked, re-read their Miranda rights and handed over to the District Attorney's assigned senior prosecutor, Alvin Goldfarb.

Al had a near-perfect conviction record in his thirty-seven years in the office. His only losses happened to be in two cases, about ten years apart, when late-provided evidence proved the defendants to be innocent.

I guess you could call that a near-perfect record.

The use of an interpreter during all interrogations was a legal requirement and was adhered to even though Al spoke almost perfect Italian after spending some "vacation" time in Sicily in 1945. After landing at the beach near Agrigento, he spent the next four months learning how to walk again at the US Army Hospital later set up near Naples.

After discharge from the Army and formal recognition for his "Beyond The Call of Duty" field service, he took advantage of the GI Bill and went to Brooklyn Law School. He graduated Magna Cum Law (or something like that) and got a prestigious appointment as a Law Clerk to Justice Black in the United States Supreme Court.

After three years, he joined the New York City District Attorney's office as an Assistant DA. Thirty-seven years later as the leading prosecutor in the office, he was handed the high profile, extremely complicated murder case that involved an international conspiracy.

His marching orders were simply stated by the DA, "Put those bastards away for a long time and make sure that full credit, along with our own boys, is also given to the Italian police's invaluable input."

After two days spent poring over all of the official papers and interviews with Connie, Franco and the Italian detectives who had accompanied the three accused during transport from Rome, Al began to chart his prosecution plan. In his usual methodical manner, he tried to envision the trial from opening to summation.

He began his trial preparation by outlining what was needed to even get to trial: international papers that would have to be presented in order to cede legal jurisdiction from Italy to his office in New York. He then jotted down the name of one of his legal assistants who spoke Italian to cover this issue and obtain said info, and to liaise with the Italian Embassy.

Similar individual assignments were then made to cover: Laticco's group input, Connie's group input including the crime scene, financial and physical forensic evidence and finally, the victim's background.

Once these assignments were made, Al began to formulate his approach to the trial. He began by listing all of the possible legal objections that would likely be raised at the very beginning by the defense team regarding international law and the right to prosecute foreign nationals in a US court.

A brief on these issues was part of the responsibility of his deputy, who was liaising with the Italian government. He was to also include a brief on precedence in similar international cases.

Al's most difficult responsibility was to establish a legal basis for prosecuting the principals behind a murder without yet having caught the actual murderer. If he proceeded with a trial at this point, what would be the effect on a subsequent murder trial once the actual murderer was in custody. Could there even be a second trial for a single murder?

He needed to do a lot of reading before asking the court for a trial date.

CHAPTER 53

Lucy had fallen asleep with tousled hair and a smile on her face, both reflected by Connie's still open eyes.

No doubt about it, he must stop off at his apartment on the way to the Precinct and get his mother's engagement ring, if he could only remember where he had hidden it. As a man of law, it was incumbent on him to make Lucy an "honest" woman, and he was determined that said path was to begin tonight.

As so often happens, life interfered with life. The best laid plans of mice and men . . . blah, blah, blah!

It was at that exact moment that he felt a vibration under his pillow and it was not Lucy!

When he had first been promoted to detective, one of the many changes to his lifestyle and habits was the elimination of a ring tone on his cell phone, to be replaced by incoming calls vibration. This was a necessary precaution in his new job. Can you imagine stalking a perp in the middle of the night and suddenly your phone starts blasting "Jingle Bells" or something like that? Bye-bye, perp, or even worse, bye-bye detective.

Hence, silent call notification.

Connie extracted the phone from its resting place and quietly slipped into the living room to take the call.

"This is Connie. Who have I got?

Yes, Ozzie, what have you got?

Good work. I should be there in less than an hour. Have the task force available!"

True to his word, Connie was standing in front of the assembled group in some fifty-seven minutes.

"OK, sip up and simmer down! Let's talk about assignments to follow up on this latest information. As you know, we now have some leads regarding the probable recent travel path and possible intentions of our killer. Ozzie, please give us a heads-up on the info you have received from our colleagues in the National Security Agency."

Ozzie picked up using the notes he had jotted down from the NSA verbal report he'd gotten earlier that morning. Using profiling leads, they'd developed an algorithm specifically based on the known facts about the perp.

"Among other characteristics, it considered a historic pattern of his alias usages. As you know, aliases are generally limited by the number of passports and bank accounts one can reasonably maintain. They picked up one alias trail that paid off like a slot machine."

"Really, Ozzie?" Connie interjected. "Like a slot machine?"

"Yes, boss. They even hit the jackpot! Using a Federal warrant and bank-provided keys, they opened a safe deposit box at New Jersey Federal Bank and Trust, in Paterson, New Jersey. Beyond nine passports from four countries, nine driver's licenses from three countries, and six major credit cards, was $580,000 in denominations lower than $100 as well as over 300,000 euro.

Better payout than a slot machine!

At any rate, they also found papers that had passwords for a Swiss bank account and two international airline accounts.

Interpol is following up on the Swiss accounts and we contacted the airlines.

From slot machine to Bingo!

Using his various known aliases, we checked the two airlines' reservations from all US and Canadian international airports to any foreign destination, and hit pay dirt. He is booked tonight at 8:30 on British Airlines from JFK to Dubai and United Airlines from Phoenix to Tokyo.

We will cover the JFK departure as well as rail and bus terminals. I have also contacted the Maricopa County Sheriff's office and they will cover Phoenix Airport and all rail and bus terminals.

He is one clever bastard, but at last we may have him boxed in!"

"What makes you think that these reservations are for real?" Connie asked. "Perhaps these are decoys and he has yet another route planned."

"I thought of that, too, boss, but it represents the only leads we currently have. I should also have mentioned that we requested the various airline, train and bus companies to check their records for departures for one month prior to, and for the next two months into the future."

Connie continued, "Please ensure that all officials are informed that operations at the various terminals are to be in plain clothes. No uniforms above those normally present. He is a master of disguise so we won't know what he will look like. We most certainly do not want to spook him before he checks in.

The rest of you will continue with your assigned investigative directions.

Questions?

Answers?

Anything?

Nothing?

Go."

Connie pulled out the thick pile of papers that had accumulated on his desk since the night before, kicked off his shoes, leaned back and started to read . . . and digest . . . and read . . . and formulated until the big AHA! moment. There was a pattern in the reports that was beginning to emerge.

The international authorities that had tried to nab Anthony were never able to find his escape route from whatever country he committed his trade in. The usual airports, RR stations, car rental agencies and freighters were fully investigated without a clue as to how he got out. Perhaps that was because he never used any of them as his escape route.

What was left?

The open sea.

Cruise ships!

His wealth was certainly there. He could certainly afford to dress well and book an exclusive cruise to anywhere his heart desired. He would likely select a smaller ship, rather than the humongous ones where they had all sorts of security to control the masses. The larger ships would expose him to too many security officers and other people, with the attendant risk of recognition.

Connie slipped on his shoes, donned his jacket and walked over to Courtyard Travel two blocks away. He found his cousin Greta at her desk and immediately bombarded her with a zillion questions.

Her answers narrowed down the possible cruise lines of interest to three, Regent, Silversea and Seabourn. Each had high-end smaller ships, each accommodating about 400 travelers.

Connie then had Greta check to see which ones had recently departed from the New York area or were scheduled to depart within the next month.

Regent was due to take on passengers the next day for its annual repositioning cruise across the Atlantic to Le Havre, France. As she explained, a repositioning cruise is when the ship is moved trans-oceanic (in this case the Atlantic Ocean) to another continent for seasonal cruises. In this particular case, the *Navigator* was due to leave Pier 53 in Manhattan at 4:00 pm tomorrow.

All aboard by 3:00 pm.

Connie immediately called the task force secretary and told her to recall the entire group back to the office post haste.

Even sooner.

He then once again made use of his extensive physical training to hightail it back within 4.62 minutes. Extensive training involved approximately three or four brews every evening while watching the box (usually his favorite, *NCIS*.)

Within thirty minutes, the entire group had reassembled, and Connie explained his plan while assigning responsibilities. They had no idea what Anthony would look like, but they had his fingerprints, previous disguises, physical abilities and limitations, personal quirks, habits, and of course, he would be a loner. The last item, loner, was very important in that they would not be looking for a couple, a group of friends or buddies, and most certainly not an extrovert.

With the help of Greta, he showed the layout of the *Navigator* to the assembled group. The ship had eleven decks, but only decks four through eight had passenger staterooms. The lower three were for the kitchen, main dining room, crew quarters, mechanical equipment, laundry and provisions storage. The top two decks were public areas (pool, dining, nightclub, etc.) and the bridge.

The bridge was that large room in the front of the tenth deck with all sorts of exotic gadgets, levers and screens, where the Captain occasionally would hang out to control the beast. The rest of the time he would change uniforms, have meals and schmooze with the guests.

Connie then appointed two-person teams, each responsible for contacting the various agencies responsible for the cruise from a passenger and operational point of view.

Lists for crew, security personnel, food and beverage suppliers, entertainers, and lading crew members, were urgently needed.

Urgent meant within two hours!

Franco was given the responsibility of alerting and liaising with the federal authorities, and Ozzie the maritime groups responsible for the port and the sailing.

Connie would head up the team to be assigned to review, modify and finally take an active role in the most likely point of entry to the vessel, the passenger boarding procedure. Connie selected five officers who had proven competence in past undercover operations, but looked "nautical," whatever that meant to him. The four men and one woman were to be outfitted with crisp new Regent junior officer's uniforms, and would be involved in the processing of all guests as they boarded.

If they could not identify their prey prior to departure, they were to stay aboard for the duration of the cruise to check luggage and other personal belongings while the guests were otherwise engaged in onshore tours or meals. Connie was confident that their quarry would most likely participate in scheduled activities to fit in with the other guests, so as not to draw attention to himself.

Connie, Franco and Ozzie would also join this group as ship's officers, should they fail to turn up their man prior to departure.

Within twenty minutes, they had confirmation from Regent that the entire ship's crew had been on board prior to the New York port of call and would remain on board for at least the next leg to Calais, France, with no replacements. Each crew member would be personally identified by his/her immediate superior.

Yes, of course they would inform Connie should that situation change at the last minute.

There was also confirmation that there was no change in their usual food or other port suppliers.

Arrangements were then made to check the identities of all longshoremen bringing goods on board. Additionally, every container would now be checked as it entered the hold by a crew member and one of Connie's officers.

CHAPTER 54

Connie and his seven officers boarded the liner at 8:00 am, and were immediately escorted to Captain DiCarlo's stateroom.

"Yes, Lieutenant, I was briefed by the CEO of our group about our little problem some thirty minutes ago. My executive officer and I are the only ones aboard with knowledge of the problem. We will obviously cooperate with you to the fullest extent, unless it jeopardizes any of our guests or crew. That, of course, is my prime responsibility.

My XO will escort you to our laundry, where the eight of you will be fitted with some of our spare replacement uniforms. Crew members that you interact with will be told confidentially that you are from our home office, checking procedures."

By noon, all eight eyed themselves in their new uniforms. Having started their careers on the beat, donning a uniform was not exactly a new experience for any of them, and they did look dreamy, gleamy and shipshape, as cruise ship officers should look.

They did not look anything like cops on the beat.

There was a briefing by the ship's XO, who outlined what their supposed responsibilities were to be. They were given a quick course in shipboard decorum. They were also told to refer guest questions about the ship to the nearest actual crew member, explaining to the guest that this was their first voyage with this particular ship.

This was followed by final postings and more specific instructions from Connie. One of them was assigned to the dockside where luggage was received as the guests left their buses or cabs. Another was assigned dockside to overview ship lading and to look out for unauthorized people and/or movements.

A male and the female officer were assigned to the check-in area where every guest was escorted to receive suite assignments, room keys, ID's and passage papers. This was also where passports were checked and then retained for the duration of the cruise. The male was to check every passport, looking for anomalies. The female officer was to be posted behind the desk doing a visual scan of every guest. Connie emphasized *every* guest, as he could be travelling as a "she"!

The remaining officers were assigned to mix with the crew, looking for the one that did not fit.

At the same time, Connie was to roam the ship watching for out-of-place behavior. This could manifest itself as extreme exclusiveness, or its opposite, gregariousness, heavy tipping to ensure privacy (even though this was one of those gratuities-included cruises), inappropriate dress, feigned inebriation or disability, etc.

Connie had ample training and experience in culling out the suspicious from a crowd.

Each officer was at his/her assigned station when the first of the guests arrived at 2:00 pm. As each guest was issued an ID card with photo printed on it, a copy of the same picture was wirelessly relayed to an officer at the central police command center. Each photo was then downloaded through multiple photo recognition databases to confirm identity.

Because most of the guests were paying piles of money for this high-end cruise, they were mostly from a cut of society that was generally well documented in the media and/or industry. As a result, most identities were confirmed within minutes. The ones that could not be found were so noted for further examination and observation.

Additionally, photo recognition checks were being run for all of the crew members, officers and men. This was accomplished by copying the ID picture of each person, comparing it to the bearer and relaying it to the liner's home office for comparison with their file photos.

Finally, all of the dockworkers, lading crew and delivery drivers were checked in a similar manner. Those had already been scanned at headquarters and had come back negative. It was a testament to modern technology that by 3:15 pm all of the non-guests had been cleared.

Connie could now redistribute all of his resources completely into the guest arena.

CHAPTER 55

Connie convened all of his people in the Captain's stateroom at 6:00 pm.

With Captain DiCarlo's help, he assigned each of his officers to a dining room table with an odd number of seated guests. Since most guests traveled as couples, the chances of a solo male guest dining at an odd numbered one was high.

The pretense of an officer joining said table was that guests would get the opportunity to interact with an officer of the ship.

Midway through dinner, each officer was to determine if anyone at the table deserved further examination and if so, nodded to Connie during his dining room rounds. After the service of appetizers, the officers would then bid goodnight to their fellow diners and visit another table with an odd number of people to expand their arena of observations.

Another officer was assigned to check which of the guests ordered room service and was to dine alone in his/her stateroom.

Connie was to roam the dining room, posing as the Guest Relations Officer, collecting information and chatting with guests who dined alone. He invited each solo passenger to the Free Spirit Mix after dinner at the observation lounge on the top deck.

Forty-three such invitations were extended. Thirty-one were women, or appeared to be at first glance. Gender would have to be confirmed by the stateroom maids.

The no-shows, along with the in-stateroom diners, would be the team's first priority.

All twelve male solo travelers, as well as the thirty-one interested females made their way to the top deck observation lounge for the Free Spirit Mix with its opportunity to extend their potential cruise relationships. Sex does not necessarily die after your mate does, you just cruise for a new mate.

The same primeval drive even applies to the over 72's, the average guest age.

What better place for such an encounter than on a "senior citizen" cruise!

High-end cruises, such as this one, are just that.

There they were, all forty-three of them, with drinks in hands, semi-lust in their hearts, and some remnant of ability in their body parts. All but possibly one neatly disguised individual had high expectations for a fun and possibly very meaningful journey.

The probability was that ten or eleven of them would couple and be off to a good start, at least for most of the next seven days and nights.

The remainder would form some sort of sisterhood that included bridge, mah jongg and an in-depth comparison of ailments, prescriptions and cardiologists. After age 75 that is affectionately called an "organ recital."

Hopefully, very hopefully, one of the remaining males would spend the rest of his time in custody awaiting a helicopter to return him to New York.

At least that was Connie's game plan.

Let the Mix begin.

CHAPTER 56

"Would you care to Cha-Cha?" the sparsely populated gray pate with matching gray hint of a beard asked of the #6-pink-tint-dyed blonde. Her billowing cloud of gelled cotton candy was set above a pair of jet-black mascara-ed dark brown eyes, all topping flaming glossy red lipstick. This entire abstract painting was ensconced on a thick pedestal of a neck, which was surrounded by a diamond-studded necklace.

Her entire upper structure was, in turn, supported by a massive pea-green silk awning enveloping a well-fed torso.

It did not take a second look to establish that almost all of the women were similarly coiffed and made-up, except for variations in colors and girth. Looking at the entire scene also confirmed that almost all of the gentlemen had identical facial hair features.

Also, the black tie/tux was obviously the requisite male guest cruise uniform.

The answer to the request for a dance was almost invariably, "I would love to." Years of "Arthur Murray teaches dancing in a hurry" went into automatic mode. If there had been an overhead camera taking in the scene, it would have looked like it came from one of the 1930's famed Hollywood cinematographers, a Busby Berkeley choreographed ballroom dancing extravaganza.

Instead of an overhead camera, Connie had arranged for one of his people to stealthily photograph each attendee and assign a number for future ID'ing and follow-up, as necessary. Pictures of all of the single travelers not attending the social mixer were also secretly shot as they were leaving the dining room.

The IDs included the women, as there was no way to predict how the perp would try to evade detection. He was obviously a master (or mistress) of the art of disguise!

Connie now faced the problem of how to photograph the in-room diners to complete the picture gallery of unaccompanied travelers.

This was accomplished by assigning one of his detectives the task of donning a dining steward's uniform and delivering the dinners. He would then use his button camera to add the additional faces to the collection. These were in turn to be compared to the ID photos taken upon initial boarding.

Not unexpectedly, all were a match.

Either they would be as previously recorded or one of them could be him, getting a bit sloppy. Hopefully, when followed up, he would forget, or would not have enough time after the knock on his stateroom door, to complete his disguise.

Except for lack of makeup and or some tousled hair, all but one were almost perfect matches. The lone exception was the gentleman who was in the bathroom during the dinner delivery, as well as the post-dinner tray pick-up.

Said gentleman later also rejected maid turndown service.

Said gentleman, later identified as Mr. Elrod Tover with an Australian passport was in Stateroom 867 on the port side eighth deck, aft amid ship.

He would require very special attention by Connie.

CHAPTER 57

Detectives Hus and Seftel were assigned to ship patrol for the night while the rest of the team geared up for a midnight visit to Stateroom 867.

Indeed, if this was their man, extreme caution and protection was a necessity. A trained assassin would not simply say, "I am all yours," and then submit to capture. Such a person had the ingrained mindset that in any situation all lives were expendable, even his own.

There would be ultimate resistance.

Kevlar vests were placed over their black incursion shirts and trousers. Face covering was not deemed necessary but all exposed skin was blackened.

The less visible the target, the less of a target it would be.

The eight team members pored over the room plan, committing to memory all potential hiding places, furnishings, clear paths, lighting and possible tripping hazards.

Detectives Hus and Seftel were assigned to the open pool Deck 9, at the railing, just above Stateroom 867. Should the perp try to escape by using his balcony to reach adjoining staterooms, he would have to shimmy over the rail, as both sides of each balcony were separated by a gate for privacy.

They were given a "shoot to kill" order should he try such an escape. His evading capture would undoubtedly lead to a hostage situation in an adjoining stateroom—to be avoided at all costs. There was no way Connie would put the lives of civilians at risk.

Incursion was planned for 2:00 in the morning, a time of least awareness and resistance.

After several rehearsals in an empty stateroom, and ensuring that each member of the team knew exactly what was expected of him, they were all ready for a Go.

Hus and Seftel left first to get in place on Deck 9. Once positioned, they were to so signify via their mics and ear buds.

"OK, John, I can see you in position via the ship's scanning camera on Deck 9. Hold until given other instructions. Remember, no one is allowed to leave the stateroom immediately below you via the balcony.

You have absolute authorization to shoot to kill."

Connie then turned his attention to the feed from Deck nine to the room incursion crew.

"Everything is in place. At my count, proceed with the entry. One, two, three . . . go!"

At the word "go," a battering ram shoved the door to Stateroom 867 in and a primed Flash Bang was tossed in. Within a millisecond all within fifty feet who were not properly protected with special dark lens glasses and ear protectors (as the team were), would experience temporary loss of vision and hearing as well as incapacitating nausea.

The team, led by Franco, was in the room just seconds after the blast. The balcony door was locked but with all of its glass blown out. All of the other glass in the room such as mirrors, tabletops, door panels, etc., were shattered. Debris was scattered throughout the room.

There was no report of anyone leaving via the balcony from John on Deck nine.

A sweep of the room found the dead body of a male in a closet. He was stripped to his underwear. His picture was forwarded to the screen on the Bridge and identified within minutes as the steward responsible for delivering dinner trays to Deck Eight. Prints lifted from some light switches were electronically sent to the bridge and run through ID programs.

Confirmation! It was their man.

A check with room service showed that the tray had been delivered about twenty minutes previously.

Obviously, the murderer was at it again, and had escaped earlier, probably dressed as the steward.

He had anticipated Connie's moves before Connie had even communicated them to his team. Being in sync was obviously a two-way street!

After they'd calmed the passengers in adjoining staterooms, they continued their check of the suite. There was no evidence in the bathroom, or elsewhere, of makeup residue or weapons.

The conclusion was that since he was not now trying to change his appearance and blend in, he was likely going to play hide-and-seek.

A new approach was urgently needed.

Connie immediately called for the four official "Dinner Companion Escorts" who in reality were the liner's undercover security team.

Since hijacking piracy had raised its ugly head about ten years ago, certain cruise ships retained such teams. This was especially true of the high-end liners where the passenger list catered to some of the more affluent travelers. Prime hostage material.

Regent was such a cruise company, and this sailing, as usual, had among its guests a large number of Bold-Faced Names. They were readily recognized for their international prominence and individual fortunes.

Connie inducted the ship's four security team members as part of his team, now numbering twelve. They were all professionals and armed.

He then outlined his plan to the assembled group, assigning each to a different area of the ship. A guard was to be positioned mid-ship on each of the passenger decks, leaving seven, led by Connie, as the search party.

He then called for the Captain and gave him a detailed picture of his plan.

The Captain was to round up all of his officers except those responsible for the bridge, kitchen and operation of other critical equipment.

Twenty of them were organized into two-man teams. The remainder were to be positioned at all entrances to the ship's theater.

The teams of two were to go to each stateroom, starting with Deck 8, the top level guest quarters. They were to then escort groups of ten guests at a time to the ship's theater. Each group of ten was also joined by one of Connie's team. The guests were to be seated and provided with refreshments while the ship's entertainers did what they could to keep the guests, well, entertained.

All of the police and security officers were provided with ear bud communication devices, automatic weapons and chest protectors.

After assignments were made by Connie, the Captain got on the PA system and broadcast the following agreed-upon message throughout the ship:

> *This is the Captain. We were notified by the New York City Police Department that there may be a person of interest to them aboard. Your wellbeing is our top priority. In order to properly control this unfortunate situation and provide for your safety, we will systematically move all of you to our theater. There you will have a secure haven, protected by our cruise and security officers. Our security personnel will escort you to the theater, stateroom by stateroom, starting with Deck 8. After Deck 8 has been cleared, we will then go to Deck 7 and follow the same procedure, deck by deck, until all of our guests have been safely escorted to the theater. I will make a PA announcement as the team of officers reaches your deck. Do not leave your stateroom or unlock your door until your deck has been announced and one of our officers knocks on your door. When you hear the knock, an officer will show a police shield at peep-hole level for ID. If said shield is not visible, do not unlock your door and immediately dial 21 on your suite phone and we will send someone to correct the situation.*
>
> *Thank you for your cooperation.*

One of Connie's officers was assigned to each deck so as to coordinate the exodus. While this was occurring, another of his officers organized the posting of an armed security person at each door to the theater, as well as a patrol of the backstage area.

A crew technician continuously scanned the room with his camera and fed it to the monitors on the bridge, which became the command center for the operation. He also relayed live activity from backstage as well as from all of the many security cameras mounted throughout the ship. This was essential for critical areas such as the engine room, the kitchen and open deck areas.

Connie, now in the command center, continuously watched the live feeds, as well as fielding questions streaming in from his agents while directing the overall action.

This case evolved from a murder discovered at the opera, where the conductor never got to the podium, to here, where Connie was now acting as the conductor in an attempt to resolve it.

Hopefully he would be more successful than the original conductor.

CHAPTER 58

Franco and his incursion team were ordered to make a complete sweep of Deck 8. This was methodically done, room by room, including all storage and maid's closets.

The utilities area on this deck offered a particular challenge to the team, as this was the center of the mechanical systems. The storage room was the heart of the swimming pool water system. It was filled with noisy pumps for water recirculation as well as for the addition of chemical additives. There was a maze of giant filters and, of necessity, storage for the very noxious chemical additives. Additionally, there were enough noise and hiding places within this confined area to create the absolute need for a very cautious approach.

The ship's engineer provided Connie with drawings of the rooms as well as a list and location within this area of all chemicals and storage crates. A team was selected, to be led by Ozzie.

Connie and Ozzie spent another precious fifteen minutes to formulate a plan of action.

The four-member team was fitted with oxygen masks in the event that a chlorine tank suffered damage causing it to leak during the incursion, and they were given their detailed assignments.

A rammed steel bulkhead door, followed by a Flash Bang, followed by a team that quickly entered and dispersed, followed by . . . nada!

It required a very precious eighteen minutes from beginning to end of the operation to ensure that Anthony was not there.

Franco and two other team members then joined Hus and Seftel on Deck 9 for a check of that deck. All enclosed spaces were uncovered, unlocked and unsealed. Airshafts, funnels and niches were totally scanned.

Again, nada.

Franco then led his team up to Deck 10, the Bridge Deck, and made sure that all areas external to the bridge, as well as the bridge itself, were clear.

Franco's team descended to successively lower decks after the guests from each deck had been transferred to the theater. They swept deck-by-deck, room-by-room and all other enclosed areas along the corridors.

When they got to Deck 4, special attention was given to the kitchens where the steward presumably was to return after his room service call.

The steward's delivery ticket for Suite 867 room service was punched in, but no one remembered seeing if he had returned from the delivery. The kitchen at mealtime was always a nonstop blur of people scurrying to and from their various workstations and responsibilities. No one ever looked up and all one really saw was just work in progress and a blur of white uniforms.

Franco's team questioned each of the 126 kitchen staff and no one was found who was not vouched for by others on duty and/or senior kitchen staff.

This was followed by a check of all kitchen areas, including refrigerators, adjacent storage areas, closets and cabinets.

While this search was going on, the guests were safely congregating in the ship's theater listening to the ten-piece band playing Beatles hits interspersed with Sinatra. The Cruise Host would introduce each selection with an attempt at a joke or an interesting fact about the ship and the sea.

Unfortunately, the fact was usually funnier than the joke and did not improve the mood. As one would expect in this type of situation, there was considerable unease among the passengers and all sorts of rumors were circulating. The noise level amplified as people loudly questioned each other. Not privy to the real reason they were assembled so hastily, there was talk about icebergs (in June?), U-Boats (WWII had been over for some

70 years), pirates, mutiny, a hole in the ship's bottom, the start of WWIII, terrorists on board, UFOs, an Ebola epidemic, etc.

"Zika?" one woman postulated. "Where would mosquitos come from in the middle of the ocean?" was the self-designated know-it-all's answer.

The Captain took Connie aside on the bridge and said, "Would it interfere with your investigation if I spoke to our guests to try to allay their fears? Not knowing is so much worse than the true situation. I believe we owe it to our passengers and our crew members to tell them what is actually happening."

Connie replied, "Yes, I agree with you, but please restrict your remarks to the theater area only. The less our prey knows about our plans, the better our chances are of resolving this with minimal damage."

The Captain, now armed and accompanied by a security man, raced down the stairs to the theater deck.

He was on stage as "I'll Do It My Way" was ending, while a disinterested audience was talking in loud distressed voices to each other.

"Ladies and Gentlemen, this is the Captain. I know that you are all feeling somewhat uncomfortable and all sorts of rumors are circulating. I want to reassure you that there is no immediate danger to anyone in this room. We are seeking an individual who is wanted for questioning by the New York City Police Department, and we have reason to believe he is on board. While he is being sought, you are extremely well protected by our professional security staff. In the interim, our catering and entertainment staff will provide you with a special dinner show.

Should you have special needs, please speak to any of the ship's officers in this room. If you are in need of medical attention and/or special medications, our ship's doctor and nurse are here to assist you. We will try our utmost to accommodate any of your special requirements to the best of our ability."

Connie ordered Franco to take his team to the ship's laundry. After all, the man had to get rid of the steward's uniform and get new duds. Where better than the laundry?

The laundry room, on Deck 2, was located aft, in a large ventilated room. Total room enclosure was necessary because of the constant noise of the washers, dryers and steam presses. As has been the custom since ocean liners first arrived, all of the laundry staff were traditionally composed of

Chinese immigrants. The original Cunard Liners, the *Queen Mary* and the *QE2* even had special Chinese food kitchens to accommodate said staff.

Should a daring guest have a "yen" for a real Chinese meal, the dining room staff was always ready to accommodate with dinner prepared in this specialty kitchen. You would have to actually travel to Beijing, or as it was originally named, Peking—as in the duck—to get a possibly better Chinese meal.

The laundry was a seven-day-a-week, twenty-four-hour operation with a staff consisting of a supervisor and eight operators. Two to tend the four huge stainless steel washing machines and six specialty combination ironing and folding machines. The latter were Rube Goldberg-like creations, whose movement defies logic. Steam and noise were a constant companion. The only times these gigantic beasts were not spewing, spinning and cranking away was when they failed or were down for scheduled maintenance. That meant that there was almost always a mechanic in the room.

Additionally, there was a linen repair alcove tended by a single day shift operator repairing torn linens.

The ship's Hotel Captain was responsible for the ship's so called "Hotel" operation and reported to the ship's Captain. He oversaw everything on board other than the movement and maintenance of the ship's propulsion. His estimate for Connie was that the crew count in the laundry room that morning should be nine.

Franco, after reviewing the ship's plan of Deck 2, led a group of four officers to the laundry room's always-closed double doors, always tightly closed because of the combination of noise, high ambient temperature and steam ever-present in the area.

The only other exit from the laundry was to the open aft deck used for storage of the ship's berthing gear.

He then determined that the best way to control the now code named "Dirty Laundry" operation was for the two officers assigned to Deck 3 (the aft informal open air dining room) to stand at the rear rail of this outdoor dining area overlooking the Deck 2 aft deck, below. This way they would have an unobstructed view of any movement there as well as potential hiding places. Also, Officer Hus, a US Army trained sniper with two tours of Afghanistan behind him, would be perfectly placed should the perp seek refuge out there.

On the count of three, the power to the laundry room was cut and the night-vision equipped team rushed in.

Six Chinese laundry room staff were lined up facing against the rear wall. To their right was the guy they were seeking, still in white steward pants and no shirt.

More importantly, he had his gun pressed against the front left temple of the laundry room crew supervisor.

Franco's cry of "Drop it!" was obviously in vain.

Instead, the coupled pair sidled toward the aft door as the assassin said in a clear, unwavering voice, "Either arrangements are made to get the two of us off this boat to a destination of my choice or this gentleman and I will both die. There is no alternative scenario."

As they went out to the deck, he continued, "Your choice."

Franco whispered into his mic, "Hus, when clear, take the shot."

CHAPTER 59

A millisecond later, Connie said, "Hus, this is Connie. Take that shot only on my authorization. I want to try something first."

Connie yelled out to the gunman, "Anthony, the man you are holding is an innocent with a large family to support. You have no quarrel with him and he is not on the hit list you were contracted for. As a professional in your field you really do not want to harm him. My name is Lieutenant Connie Collins of the New York City Police Department. I am the man you really want in front of your gun. With your agreement, I will take his place. Let this be a problem for professionals to sort out."

You could almost hear the simultaneous jaw-dropping as all of Connie's team immediately realized that this was Connie, Jr., son of Connie, the legendary NYPD negotiator.

Déjà vu.

However, Connie did not get that opportunity to follow in his dad's negotiating footsteps.

While all were distracted by Connie's courageous stance, Anthony pushed his hostage aside and jumped into the ocean. A startled Hus began firing away at the area where Anthony hit the water.

After a good five minutes, there was no telltale blood pool or body in the water.

The Captain immediately dispatched a lifeboat manned by his crew, with Connie and Hus on board for protection. After thirty minutes of searching a large perimeter around the ship of seemingly unending ocean, there was still no evidence of a body. Though logic pointed to his demise, the lack of said body dictated the only logical conclusion to be incorporated in Connie's yet-to-be-written final report. "Because of no physical evidence of survival and lack of a body, the perpetrator was deemed to be lost at sea."

Standoff ended, innocent hostage unharmed, passengers and crew saved without further injury, and the City of New York saved a ton of money by not having a lengthy trial.

Dead bad guys do not need earthly trials.

They get theirs elsewhere.

CHAPTER 60

"Miss Marker," the voice Elaine recognized as that of her security chief. "You have some visitors who have been cleared for entry. May I admit Attorney Welling, Lieutenant Connie Collins and Sergeant Franco D'Angelo?"

She gave her approval and the door was remotely unlocked by the agent on duty in the control room.

The three entered the room, all preceeded by giant smiles radiating at least two feet in front of them.

No sales spiel for teeth whiteners needed here.

Their gleaming faces told her the entire story in a millisecond.

After weeping with joy, the hugs, and the need for her to sit for a moment, Connie relayed the story of the ending of the threat to her life and to her unborn child.

More weeping and more hugs.

Welling then picked up the narrative. "By agreement with the Italian authorities, the Prince's three former associates will be tried in the Fourth Circuit Federal District Court in New York City on murder conspiracy charges. If convicted, they will serve their term in US Federal prisons. If not convicted, or upon their ultimate release from said prison, they will be returned to Italy to face a trial based on their numerous financial crimes.

In any event, they will likely spend their remaining years incarcerated here or abroad."

Welling continued, "As regards your child's inheritance, we have concluded our financial analysis of the Prince's bequest. A reasonably conservative estimate of what will be transferred to the account which you will have full control over until your child's 21st birthday is approximately four billion four hundred million US dollars, give or take several hundred million.

Of course, there will be inheritance taxes of about 25% to be paid, but the remaining three billion plus should be enough to live on. That is, if you do not plan to buy Monaco or another small country."

After thanking Mr. Welling some six thousand times, Elaine discussed retaining Welling et al to continue as her solicitors. She also started preliminary arrangements to buy the condo she was presently ensconced in.

Most importantly to her, she received permission to once again contact her relatives, her voice coach Mme. Kordavanska and, of course, the Metropolitan Opera.

A new stream of life was about to begin.

After Welling's departure, Connie, Franco and Elaine, now joined by Lucy, went out for a celebration dinner –for the first time in close to four weeks without an armed escort.

To add a dollop of whipped cream to the finale, she asked Connie if he would consider leaving the Department and head up her personal security team, all of his choosing. Obviously, Ozzie would be offered a key position on the team.

Connie's annual salary would be well over $1, 000,000/year, for life. His team would also not be financially hurting.

Not such a bad future for soon-to-be-former New York City cops!

Not such a bad future for the prospective Met star soprano!

EPILOGUE

You didn't think that this saga would end so abruptly, did you?

Try to think realistically.

First of all, Prince Emanuel was properly buried, with a day of national mourning to commemorate his status, humanity and reputation as a noted generous philanthropist.

The three Italian bad guys were sentenced by a NYC court to twenty-to-forty years each for their role in causing and paying for the murder of a US citizen on US soil. If still alive, upon release, and by agreement with the Italian authorities, they would be returned to Italy to stand trial for their role in the forging of the Prince's financial documents and his will. The likelihood was that they would never see daylight again without peering through bars.

Now on to the future of our NYC friends.

What about Franco? you ask.

Good question!

The constant interpersonal security relationship between Elaine and Franco led to a more permanent and extremely personal relationship.

Life had to move on beyond the tragedy that had introduced them to each other.

I'll bet that you were not fully aware of this growing attraction. She was obviously very attracted to men of Italian heritage and he was absolutely smitten by her.

Would you turn down the opportunity to marry a gorgeous and extremely talented woman who has fallen in love with you and you love and who also just happens to have inherited some three billion dollars (after taxes)?

Of course, Franco promptly resigned from the NYC police department. Dedicated to the department?

Yes!

Crazy?

No!

Franco figured that among other things, he could now afford imported gelato for the rest of his life.

Elaine's singing lessons with Madame Kordavanska were delayed one year so that they would have the time to get married—yes, married—and deliver a healthy and robust young Enrico into this world.

A very formal July wedding at the Ringwood Country Club, which Elaine had recently bought as a fun investment, was attended by:

all of her Indiana family
Mr. Welling, Connie, Lucy, Ozzie
half of the midtown NYC Police Force
the management and principal conductor of the Metropolitan Opera
Detective Lattico and his crew (all flown over in Elaine's private jet)
four hundred guests in all.

Even the weather cooperated and yes, of course, the dessert was stracciatella gelato specially imported for the occasion from Rome.

Elaine's condo was certainly large enough to require and house the necessarily large staff.

Key were the butler and the nanny.

An extended search found Stephan, who had dedicated his life to Service. They then brought in a Mary Poppins-like woman (actually her name was Nanny Murdoch).

With Stephan seeing to the functioning of the home, Nanny in charge of little Enrico, and Connie aided by Ozzie overseeing the security aspects, Elaine and Franco felt comfortable enough to start planning their two-month world tour/honeymoon.

Not a bad life for an ex-cop and a Renee Fleming wannabe.

Ozzie, with Elaine's additional help, immediately remitted sufficient funds to bring his entire extended remaining family from Sudan to New York and set them up with apartments, furnishings and jobs. The younger ones were provided with catch-up education and future higher education trusts.

His very comfortable position and salary as Connie's assistant in Elaine's security detail paid more than enough to allow for a very comfortable and secure lifestyle when not working.

All he needed was a woman to share this with.

He was working on this.

Now on to Connie.

Connie finally took the penultimate step toward making Lucy an honest woman with a long overdue proposal of marriage.

The Ringwood Country Club was made available to them by Elaine for their wedding. Not quite as elaborate as Elaine and Franco's, some three months earlier, but certainly just as beautiful and with many of the same guests returning for this much-anticipated union.

They had a delayed their honeymoon so that they could join Elaine and Franco six months later on board her private jet for a joint, two-month honeymoon/vacation.

Have I forgotten anything?

Oh yes, as if that were not enough of a happy ending, Franco bought a renowned chain of Italian gelaterias, Omnia Stracciatelli.

Now THAT'S a delicious ending!

-END -

ABOUT THE AUTHOR

Edward Gray is a retired chemical engineering executive. A father and grandfather, he lives in Connecticut with his artist wife, Barbara.

Made in United States
North Haven, CT
27 February 2022